I0236543

Time is on the Second Floor

Daniel Chambers

To those who raised me
To those who carried me
And to those who guide me

Preface

"Daniel, it's as if all of life and existence is this grand city with all sorts of experiences to be had with laughter, love, sadness, and every emotion to feel. Yet you stand on the outskirts of life and stare into the void of death pondering what is out there instead of what is to be experienced here."

My counselor told me this during one of my bouts of depression and suicidal thoughts. It almost has a harsh tone as he explained to me how he thought my depression worked. What he said in this short quote is that I seem to be obsessed with the afterlife and what it could hold. I often times expressed that the idea of whatever is after death is equivalent to those old explorers looking for new lands and mapping out the Earth. Death, too, is unexplored territory.

My obsession with death did not come from depression; rather, my depression came from an obsession with death. When I say "death", I do not mean the act of death in the gothic connotation of the word. I have never been interested in the act of death itself but rather the mystery of what happens to the conscious being upon its physical ending. No doubt you're thinking of what the answer could be as you read about my pondering of the afterlife. Someone out there could be thinking about how wonderful it will be to reunite with God. Another stranger is possibly thinking how ridiculous it is to believe anything at all happens; the body shuts down and so does our consciousness.

I have no say in which is true and which is not. However, another person's answer does not influence or sway what I think could be beyond the curtain. Why? Because we're all on this side of the curtain. Each person on Earth has their thoughts and faith about what could happen after death with every person believing or knowing that their perspective is the right perspective. This is what makes it so incredibly curious for me, so I shifted my idea of questioning from a place of sadness or depression to that of inquiry. I do not hate the grand city standing behind me and love to join in it's vast expanse of experiences, but what is out there beyond the city of life? What lies behind the curtain we all must walk through? Will I be met with pearly gates and a line of people waiting to enter? Will I be met with torturous demons who will rip apart my soul for eternity? Maybe I will die and have no knowledge of anything happening because I will simply be no more.

I woke up at 1:30 a.m. one morning with a dream still fresh in my mind. There was nothing incredibly different about this night, and even the dream that woke me wasn't some profound revelation. In the dream I found myself standing inside what resembled the long hallway of a Community Center. There's no doubt that you've probably seen the type of place I'm describing. They are large buildings which normally hold public meetings, events, or (in the case of my dream) a place to cast votes.

In front of me there were people looking at a piece of paper in their hands. Looking down at my own hand, I found the same piece of paper. It was a ballot. This ballot listed every religion (that I knew of at least) and had a small box next to it to cast my vote. At the front of the line was a large black curtain each person would walk behind. It didn't look as if we had any choice but to cast our vote and to walk behind the curtain. I quickly realized that the ballot was to vote on what we thought could be behind the curtain.

Some people in line were desperately trying to convince others that their vote was the right one. Others were mocking people for voting a certain way. But here we all were, on this side of the curtain absolutely obsessed with this answering the question, "What is behind the curtain?" My mind was rife with confusion. Why were we all standing in this line? Why do we have this ballot? Does my vote matter? What's behind the curtain? Why can't I just leave the line?

I sat up in my bed and thought about my dream for a moment. At first I simply thought it was just an interesting concept and promptly went back to sleep. The next few weeks I pondered the dream and its implications. At the time I was in the middle of publishing my first book but kept expanding on this small idea born from a very short dream.

What if death wasn't this thing where our bodies stopped working but was a giant curtain we had to walk through? How would our beliefs change? Are our beliefs nothing but votes we cast on a ballot never knowing if they have any meaning? The foundation of these questions kept spiraling but ultimately originated with one question. Why do we believe what we believe?

Is there a God? Is there a heaven or hell? What are morals? Why should I believe this philosopher over this other philosopher? What is truth? What do we know and what do we only believe? I think the answer may surprise each of us. But who knows, maybe I only believe that and don't know that.

Time is on the Second Floor is a book that kept tapping its foot in the back of my mind waiting to be written. There is only one purpose to this story and it is to make you think heavily on your existence, beliefs, God, and death. It's a book which explores every existential question I've had in my life. My hopes is not to burden any person with an existential crisis but to show a different perspective of existence and in the end have you questioning your own foundations.

With this preface I ask only these things of you: keep seeking, keep asking questions, and please remember that time works differently on the first floor.

Contents

The Road Most Travelled

1

An Ominous Beauty

12

The Third Floor

32

Green Grass and Dark Fabric

43

Chicken Fingers

56

A Puzzling Encounter

73

The Rabbit and the Bear

85

Freely Chosen or Chosen Freely

92

A Much Needed Guide

103

Through the Corridor

121

An Atheist and a Christian

136

From Eternity to the Beginning

148

The Story of a Soul

162

A Father Meets His Son

168

The State of Being

175

God and Church

184

The Guilty Pay

196

A Sandwich and Liquor

206

A Talk in front of Darkness

217

Finishing a Book

229

Wake and Wander

242

A Child finds Evil

254

The Most Powerful Being

264

Nods and Sighs

278

The Years to Come

286

Into the Unknown

296

Chapter I

The Road Most Travelled

A young man sits on a bus upon which he never entered. His name is Thomas, but most call him Tom. After all, this is how he would normally introduce himself. Tom would be a tall man of roughly six-foot one inch. His physique would mimic a fresh pear with a relatively thin shaped torso leading down to his intrusive gut hanging over his brown laced belt. His hair, I think, will be flat with little curls arching upward at the tips. His skin would be pale like sour milk and unpleasant until one gets to know him better and sees Tom as a pearl.

But what do you think? I'm describing a man who doesn't have much going for him at surface level. Of course, only perceived by his peers mind you. Personally I don't see all the fuss about someone's physical appearance but here I am, describing a man who we all probably have seen at one point. The character of Tom isn't truly affected by his outward appearance other than the clothes he would wear.

Oh, shoot. I forgot to mention his clothes. No doubt you're imagining a nude man sitting on a bus right now. We obviously can't have Tom waltzing around nude for the entire book. Let's give him a collared shirt covered by a light blue sweater. I like the idea of a brown laced belt around his waist holding up a pair of khaki pants meeting nicely tailored shoes. There, much better. I think Tom will look rather nice in the Community Center.

The Community Center? Drat, I wasn't supposed to mention the Community Center until much later. I promise I won't spoil anything else. I'll keep my mouth shut about the Community Center for now if we want to just keep watching Tom. Agreed? As if I can hear you agree. But I'll pretend you did. After all, we're going to get to the end of the book eventually. I mean, Tom can't remain asleep on the bus forever. I wouldn't be doing anyone any favors if the entire book our protagonist was only asleep on the bus.

Tom wasn't asleep on the bus for long, so no need to worry. Although, he couldn't remember anything before waking up on the bus. This was no surprise to anyone who'd ever been on this particular bus. No matter who woke up on the bus, no one remembered how they got there. It was a terrible case of amnesia. But is it really amnesia if they never had memories in the first place? I know, you're not understanding the full picture yet. Much like Tom, you're waking up to this book a little confused about where it's going to take you and how you're going to get there. You're probably a little curious but are holding out judgement until you learn a little more about the place you're in.

As luck would have it, Tom is in a similar position. You see, Tom didn't exist until right now in this moment. Neither did any other passenger as they sped across the dirt road. All adorable people who would soon be introduced to the amazing expanse known as existence. Within, of course, the Community Center that I mentioned earlier. Roughly twenty to thirty people all sitting in their place as the bus rolls along to its destination. They'll all experience problems and hardships, good times and lovely moments of life. Hopefully, they'll come around and rise to the occasion of each moment. But I focus on Tom because he's the one who has truly intrigued me for a while now.

Me? The author? No, I'm not the author. I'm not in some weird twist *you* either. Thank goodness I'm not you either. You and I both know you have a list of your own problems that could be reserved as a book all on its own.

So, who am I? More accurately would be "what am I?" I think. Because I'm not something necessarily human. But I have been in your shoes before. It'll make sense eventually, I promise. Right now, I am the thing inside your head listening to the words you are reading. I've been with you your entire life actually. I've seen everything you've ever done. Yes, I've even seen the things you keep to yourself in the dark crevices of your mind. I can prove it too!

Picture in your mind an apple. Do you see the apple? Well, no. You don't physically see the apple. Who saw the apple? Was it you? No, because it's not physically there in front of you. It's an apple inside your thoughts. You created the apple in your mind. I saw the apple! I'm the eyeballs in your mind who saw the apple! It looks pretty good. I've honestly seen better though. Now, take a moment away from this book and scream as loud as you can in your head. Easy, not that loud. I'm the ears who heard you screaming in your head. Relax, it was just a thought experiment. But anyway, nice to meet you officially. I'd shake your hand, but I'm stuck inside your mind unfortunately. I've never really ventured past the infinite walls of your mind. Although I do always try my best to get you *ahead* in life. Little mind humor for you. You can have that for free. Want to get back to Tom? Yeah, I get it. Where were we. Ah, yes, Tom's sandwich.

We weren't talking about his sandwich? We're still on the bus? Man, you are really slow. I expected us to be at the end already. Can we just skip to the end? What's so exciting about learning about a thirty-one-year-old man waking up by the jolting of a bus bouncing up and down on an unpaved road? Tom (our soft and pudgy friend) wakes up not remembering anything before this specific moment. He looks around and sees other people waking up also. He quickly notices similarities between himself and the other passengers, or so he thinks. As far as Tom knows and understands what little he does, they look like him. He looks down and sees two hands, two legs, a torso, and clothes draped over his body (you remember his clothes, we talked about them earlier). Looking around, Tom could see the other passengers having similar appendages just like him. The man sitting directly to Tom's right looked to be a little more startled than most other people on the bus. Other than the fear in his eyes, Tom saw the same basic features in the man. His clothes looked very different from Tom though. He wore a black shirt with no patterns of any kind with cargo shorts. His hair looked greasy and untidy as if the man didn't care about the way he was presented at all.

Tom's concentration was suddenly broken from the man sitting next to him. The bus hit another large hole causing Tom to bounce slightly. His eyesight caught the front of the bus where a woman stood maintaining balance with each bump of the road. The woman didn't look cruel or unpleasant to Tom, but she carried authority as she checked something off her clipboard. The sound of her writing utensil felt almost louder than the bus itself as she made her check marks. Her clothes looked slightly different than everyone else's. She wore a blue uniform fitting perfectly to her curved sides. The uniform included a small, slightly darker blue tie, and dark shorts. She had something on her head Tom didn't recognize to be anything at all. He assumed her head was just oddly shaped like a disc. But Tom did notice how he felt about her. He felt as though this woman was *more* than him if we were to ask him. But what Tom describes is what you and I know as "authority". Tom felt the woman had authority in the bus.

The stranger sitting next to Tom felt as though he should speak with the woman about the current predicament he found himself in. He stood to his feet and slowly walked down the middle aisle. The bumps of the road shook him about as he grabbed the sides of the seats occasionally. People sitting down didn't know how to react. They could do nothing but sit still until his imbalance knocked into them. Still, the people didn't know how to react as they were new to existence. Tom looked behind him to get a better look at some of the passengers. They all stared at the strange man making his way up the aisle to the woman in uniform. She stared at the man and his attempt reach the front of the bus. She looked as if she knew the entire time what the man would say to her.

Tom looked closer at some of the passengers. The bus was completely full. Everyone looked to be around the same age as Tom. The bus was a mixture of men and women of all variety. Some of the men had long stringy hair and some of the women had short spiky hair. Some people were rather large and some of them looked only to be skin and bones. Tom noticed a woman who noticed him also. She quickly looked away, but Tom kept staring at her. He noticed the moment she looked away, her face turned a shade of red. Tom, unfortunately, was too preoccupied with the sudden burn in his chest to really think about her face turning red. You and I know this sensation as attraction. His eyes averted from the woman and he looked at other people hoping she didn't notice. His eyes darted to another person on the bus who quickly put out the burning sensation in his chest, but Tom didn't understand why. He greatly wanted to meet all the strangers collected on the bus. Every person looked as interesting as the last regardless of any burning sensation in his chest. Every person unique and different who he wanted to understand. But one thing every person did have in common, was a face of confusion painted across them.

Tom sat back down in his seat and looked toward the front. He sees the man who sat next to him now reaching the woman in uniform. The man and woman inaudibly spoke to one another until she promptly made a gesture. She extended one of her fingers to where Tom sat. The man turned his head and slowly made his way back to the seat he originated. Tom could see the worry and distress his eyes as he plopped back down. Tom wondered about what the man asked the woman.

Can I just say, before I move any further, this is really a drag for me? I understand you don't see the story as I've seen it because this is the first time you've picked up this book. But I am, this book. It's like remembering the flashes of memory when you went to school for the first time. Somehow, through all the mess of life and heartache, these memories are supposed to come full circle in the end. Is that subtle enough foreshadowing for you? Maybe I'm so intrigued with Tom because his entire existence isn't about ignoring the curtain but attempting to understand it.

Uh-oh, I mentioned something else you're not supposed to know about until later. Great, now I'm spiraling. You see, I knew this would happen. The minute you picked up this book I knew I would get overly excited about the Community Center, the curtain, and especially the sandwich. Oh man, it is a good sandwich too. The bread, the honey ham, crunchy chips, and the mustard all together forming a perfect sandwich. Did I mention the mustard? Ah, yes, I did mention it. You've got to have mustard on your honey ham sandwich. It's hardly a sandwich without it. Tom understood that, but we'll get to the end of the story eventually (spoiler alert, it ends with a sandwich... kind of).

Alright, get a hold of yourself. Not you the reader. I'm talking to myself. Let's get this going again.

The woman stood at the front of the bus and gave a long speech about welcoming the group to existence.

You want to hear exactly what she said? That'll be tough. Not even Tom remembers everything she said. I barely remember everything she said. But it should be coming up in a few more sentences. So, I think we'll get the whole memory in a moment if you just keep reading. Yes, I see it just down there. Wait for it, okay, here she is.

"Welcome to existence. My name is Irene. I've existed for roughly one year now. That probably doesn't make a whole lot of sense to most of you, but I assure you, things will slowly clear up. The one thing I need you to do right now is remain calm. Most of you look to be keeping your heads on straight pretty well...," she said looking at everyone on the bus. Her eyes rested with disapproval on the man sitting next to Tom. These aren't things Tom, or the man noticed. No one sitting on the bus had any knowledge of what disapproving was or what social cues meant. They simply sat and listened to her speak. "...in a moment your minds will be flooded with countless bits of information. None of it is crucial to the Community Center. But it will help you when interacting with your fellow citizens. Subjects like math, physics, who you are, your personality, etcetera...," she continued. The woman pointed to her head as a clue for where the mind was. This small gesture let Tom and the rest of the passengers know what his mind was, and where it was. He looked up to try and see his mind but couldn't see anything but the ceiling of the bus. He looked back to the front to see what Irene was doing but she continued only touching her head looking at the passengers. Tom glanced around and saw just about everyone else was looking up just as he had. He felt a little less embarrassed now and smiled knowing he wasn't the only one who tried the same thing, except for the man next to Tom. The strange man didn't seem to have any interest in what Irene had to say. He only tapped his foot nervously on the floor of the bus. Tom watched the man, growing a sense of fear in himself. Another sensation he wasn't accustom to and didn't understand. There was nothing for Tom to fear, so what was it about this man making

Tom so anxious? Drips of sweat fell down the man's neck and he wouldn't keep his eyes off the seat in front of him.

"...the Community Center houses about one thousand people give or take. It really depends on the day," Irene told the passengers, snapping Tom out of his trance. He quickly looked up unaware if he missed any part of the speech.

Oh, that's not good. If Tom missed a part of the speech, that means we missed a part of the speech. And if we missed a part of the speech then who knows how it will affect the story.

I'm sure it's fine. Don't even worry about it. I mean, how important could her speech actually be? It's only about all existence and what to expect. It's fine. We'll be fine.

"...People are constantly coming and leaving but overall, we generally stay around the same population. Along with the general knowledge of existence, you'll be given a pretty basic idea of morals. Now, these include things like no stealing or killing. If you don't feel the sense of morals come over you please inform me before you leave. I already know you won't, but it would be much easier on the rest of us if you did. We all live in the Community Center and no one wants to ruin it for anyone else...," she said as she mimicked killing for the passengers. He didn't know what either stealing or killing were yet, so he wasn't able to tell if her mimic was of stealing or killing. He knows that she took a jacket from the woman sitting in the front seat of the bus and held it up like it were her own, then quietly gave it back to the woman. But Tom didn't worry since she said he would understand more in a moment.

"...the entire experience lasts as long as you do. Normally a couple of years and then you'll head towards the center....," she told everyone.

Tom wondered what was at the center of the Community Center and why he would one day head there. What was so important? Was it whatever he missed during his trance with his seat neighbor? He glanced back at the strange man; he was still anxious from everything.

"...Lastly, you'll be given this....," she said holding up a rectangular piece of paper. Tom couldn't make heads or tails of what was written on it. "...This is your ballot. This holds every belief that has ever been held in the Community Center. You can mark at any time what it is you believe in. Every belief is given a small description of itself but if I were you, I would start by finding someone with that belief to explain more clearly what it entails. The beliefs are listed in order of how many people believe....," she put the ballot onto her seat and looked to the driver Tom hadn't noticed until now. The driver was obscured by a wall of some sort, but Tom could just make out the figures blue jacket and an odd shaped head like Irene. She nodded her head and looked back to the curious passengers. "...And with that, we will soon be arriving at the Community Center. I'm very excited for you all. We still have about fifteen minutes. Enjoy the knowledge that slowly comes to you and become acclimated with your new minds. And... try to relax," she concluded her speech with a large smile. Tom wondered what Irene was just about to say before the bus driver cut her off. Something about the way the beliefs are listed on the piece of paper.

But, for whatever reason, Tom trusted Irene and her judgement. She was in charge. He didn't feel an attraction for her like the woman who sat behind him. He felt a slow burn of warmth fill his body as he felt he was safe. She welcomed him with a lovely smile, and he was happy to have his first experience in existence. The man next to him was another story. A story Tom worried would ruin his own.

Chapter II

An Ominous Beauty

Tom leaned his head against the window at the conclusion of Irene's speech. For a moment, he ignored the man sitting next to him and attempted to think. It was really only that, an attempt to think. You didn't misread, Tom simply tried to think for the first time. Thinking is something we do every day and yet never really understand. Sure, we can turn to the science of it all and understand the electrical patterns in our brain showing us a map of our thoughts. But in your own mind, in that place, thoughts are difficult to think about in the context of something new. Tom, for instance, has thought the entire time he's been awake. What do I mean by "think"? Is Tom's existence simply to think? I'd *think* not. That's another mind pun for you. Okay, moving on.

Animals can think. Computers can think. Who knows, maybe plants can think albeit on a different plane of existence unperceivable to human senses. Tom already knew how to think. What Tom learned now was that he understood that he was thinking. As he stared outside the bus window, his breath fogged the bit of glass in front of his mouth, he started to understand thinking. He now understood everything I've described to you in regard to thinking. Tom understood he was on a bus. He understood he was headed to a place called the Community Center. He saw his faint reflection in the glass and understood it was him. The breath fogging up the window Tom understood to be his own breath and the air he needed to remain in existence. He attempted to grasp that he was now a being who existed. In one word, Tom was given, consciousness.

"It's nighttime," Tom thought to himself. Something I haven't mentioned to you, but Tom could clearly see outside the bus as he watched the darkness. He now understood what nighttime was. And even more important (in my opinion) he knew something you didn't know. He knew something about the story I didn't even know until it was revealed. There are things in the story the characters of the book understand more than you or I ever will. It's up to the characters to share them with us.

Tom's thoughts built atop one another. He knew night would soon turn into day and the cycle would continue into a week, into a month, and eventually a year. The lights from the bus illuminated the sides of the lumpy dirt road to reveal passing trees. Tom understood the illuminating lights and what a dirt road consisted of. He looked at the passing trees, long slender slabs of wood growing green leaves only feet from the bus. This was another piece of knowledge Tom suddenly knew. His mind was learning new bits of information continuously. Tom grinned. Learning became a sense of pleasure he loved experiencing. It was as if his lack of knowledge was a deep ocean he wanted to continually explore. As he dove into the depths, he found pieces of knowledge that only unraveled more mysteries begging to be found. Tom looked below at the seat he sat on. He now saw the blue pattern with yellow and colorful splashes of confetti spread across it in wonderful design. He didn't much care for this sporadic pattern. But he found beauty in understanding more about himself as he looked around.

Just so you're aware about the writing style of this book, it won't cover a lot of detail you're probably used to in large novels. For example, the story won't go into the history of the bus. It won't describe the exact label of clothing Tom is wearing. It never even mentioned his haircut for you. These details are found in a lot of books to paint a larger picture of the world being presented, but this story is tightly focused around the things that seem appropriate for the moment they are in. For example, the buses history could very well play a role in the story and role in the Community Center. But then it would take away from more engaging parts of the story. Like a certain sandwich Tom ends up eating in the end. It really is a great sandwich. But I digress. Onward! Into the unknown of the story!

Taking in all the information, Tom sat in his chair feeling much smarter than he was before. His eyes suddenly widened a bit at the realization of a sudden piece of knowledge that materialized in his head. This piece of knowledge wasn't a personality trait, or an external understanding. No, it was Tom's name. It stood amongst the other thoughts in his mind, those thoughts giving his character substance as the label of who he was. No, this was his label. He now knew his first name was Thomas. A few moments later and he knew he was not just any Thomas. He was Thomas Lewis. He pondered on the name for a moment. Shortening the two names, he whispered under his breath "Tom Lew," which was not an incredibly pretty name. It didn't role off the tongue as he hoped, but the name Tom was simple enough to remember. He found it particularly handy that people could now decipher between himself and other "Toms" by using his last name. In time, the embarrassing moment of being mistaken for another Tom, would fade away and his obsession with whatever was behind the curtain would overtake his thoughts. In time, many things would happen that won't happen in the narrative of this story. In *time*, things would be more linear than Tom would experience them. But that's for another chapter soon to come.

Tom glanced at the person sitting next to him again hoping to see if the adventure of learning calmed him down at all. But, unfortunately, the man seemed even more anxious than before. The constant flood of information looked like small drums beating on the inside of his poor skull. The man scrunched up his face and shook his head every so often to try and rattle the drums off balance. It was as if he were in a great deal of pain from their incessant playing. None of the information flooding into Tom's head indicated to him that he knew this person. He didn't recognize him in any way. Not that Tom would understand the sensation of recognizing someone yet anyway. Tom didn't know anyone to recognize yet, or so we think.

The man wore glasses he kept pushing back onto the brim of his nose. His left hand gripped tightly around his knee bouncing up and down in rhythm against the spontaneous bounces of the bus. The only obvious conclusion Tom could come to was that the man was nervous about their arrival to the Community Center. Tom felt a new sensation in his chest called pride as he came to this conclusion. Deducing from his surroundings as to why the man was afraid made Tom feel intelligent in the moment. Intelligence was a feeling he wanted to replicate as often as possible in the Community Center.

He thought it was strange for the Community Center to be something the man would be anxious about. Everyone on the bus had the same amount of knowledge as everyone else. Simple knowledge given to them like who they were and where they would be. Everything in Tom's mind was laid out neatly for him. He knew he needed food for eating and drinks for hydration. He knew where to find these things in the Community Center as well. He knew where clean stations were so he could shower and maintain his body. Looking around, Tom could see every other person was learning as well. He saw the young woman he was attracted to at first. She smiled staring at something in her hand that glowed across her face. Tom didn't know what it was but wasn't concerned. She looked like she was enjoying learning about existence. The only one who Tom didn't understand was the man sitting next to him. The man who was not interested in any part of the Community Center it seemed.

"What's going on?" Tom leaned over with a small grin asking the man. This startled him.

Which him? Both the man and Tom actually. Tom had never spoken before. His vocal chord's vibrated in a wonderful noise escaping his mouth. It was truly something amazing he didn't know he would ever get used to. Touching his own throat, Tom made a few high and low noises feeling the vibration. The man only watched, as Tom smiled greatly experimenting with his new voice. This made the stranger feel even more uncomfortable. Tom's smile disappeared and he quickly lowered his hand.

"What's going on? You okay?" Tom asked, dropping his voice lower covering the awkward smile he was just caught having.

"Nothing. I'm fine. It's fine," the man said frantically attempting to keep his composure. He stopped looking at Tom and stared at the front of the bus where Irene and the bus driver sat.

Tom looked away and wondered about the type of person he was going to be. He wondered about the type of person he was, specifically in this type of situation. Tom wanted to be a relaxed type of person. He wanted to be the type of person who would live a happy and joyous existence with no problems to be found. So, his first decision in existence, was to share this profound relaxation with his newfound neighbor.

The first thing Tom didn't understand was why this man was so nervous about new beginnings. Tom loved trying new things and wanted to see exactly what the Community Center was. He was excited to accept the reality presented to him and live happily. Tom was very excited to check off whatever belief he would subscribe to and even share it with his family and friends. Maybe, just maybe, Tom could transform this man's anxiety to a little bit of excitement also.

"It's alright. We're all in this together," he told the man as relaxed as possible. The stranger did not share in the phenomena Tom had of being relaxed. His leg continued to bounce wildly as he continued to stare at the back of Irene's head who also looked very relaxed. She also looked at something very bright in her hand lighting up her face. Tom kept staring at Irene to figure out what the small object in her hand was, but as he did, he learned something new, something peculiar. He saw Irene, but he had no idea what she was thinking. Tom could only know the thoughts of his own mind.

Not knowing what other people were thinking would be a hurdle Tom thought he would have to get used to.

Between you and me, it's something he'll probably forget about pretty soon. I mean, how often do you go around wondering if you can read people's minds?

A lot? Point taken. I'll take that into consideration next time I read a book with you.

"I need to ask her if I can go back. There must be a way out of this," he suddenly told Tom. The man kept staring forward, as if Tom wasn't there. Tom didn't share in the "go back" phenomena the man was experiencing. Tom hadn't given much thought at all about where they came from. Taking a glance out the window, Tom assumed they came from somewhere extremely forest-y if the surrounding environment was anything to go off. Looking forward again, Tom saw Irene shuffle in her seat a little to get more comfortable as she stared at the object in her hand.

"She looks pretty calm. I think if she's okay with all of this then we're probably safe," Tom told the stranger. He could tell the man wasn't buying Tom's attempt at comfort. Paranoia was clearly overwhelming him. The man simply couldn't remain calm in the situation. It was as if he could only see what he convinced himself of, everything was working against him. Tom saw in the man's face that he only focused on this thought.

"How can you trust her? How can you trust any of this? We don't know. We don't know what's going on here. What if it's all a lie?" he furiously told Tom. This line of questioning from the man forced Tom into a whirlwind of questions himself. Sure, Tom was given knowledge of where they were going and the basics of existence, but did he really have any inkling as to what any of it was?

Staring at Irene with the stranger, Tom contemplated the questions presented to him. Unlike the man's questioning though, Tom saw them from a different perspective. Anxiety didn't rush over him like it did with the man. Tom saw the questions as any other question he would come across. He saw them as unexplored areas of his mind. But the man could not see it this way. When the man questioned something he saw it only as doubt and uncertainty. And if there was uncertainty, then there was potential for harm.

If the man were right, and everything Tom experienced was a lie, then who could he trust and what was to be gained from the Community Center? Could Tom even trust his own thoughts being fed to him? What an interesting point. As I said before, I am the thing in your mind listening to the words you're reading. So how can you trust who *I* am, and I am reading it correctly? Are you actually reading? Or am I the one reading to you? That's okay. Tom didn't want to think too deeply into it either.

"Why would you want to go back?" Tom asked the man still motionlessly staring at Irene with him. The man leaned over to Tom and spoke with a quiet whisper.

"If we're here, then that means where we've been must be safe. It's the only fact I can think of. I could go back and... just be safe," the man said. Tom was not so sure if this were the case though. The man leaned back and sat straight forward. Tom allowed the man's assumptions to bounce around his head. Both the man and Tom concluded they weren't even sure if the bus they sat on was safe. And this business of existence was a mystery on its own. There was no way to tell if any of this situation was an absolute truth. But also, who was to say whatever was before the bus wasn't any more a lie than where they currently were?

As if Tom could see how deep the rabbit hole went, physically in front of him, he decided not to tug at the questioning of what was true and what wasn't. He didn't want to spend all his existence thinking about these questions like the man clearly was. So, Tom only held onto the one question instead of venturing down the dark rabbit hole. The question of whether there was an absolute truth.

Looking to the man, Tom decided to keep this question to himself. He could tell the man found a slight bit of solace in the idea that where he had been before existence was safe. But Tom didn't enjoy these questions at all. The thoughts of not trusting anyone made him uncomfortable. He didn't know what exactly he would experience at the Community Center, but he had faith in the idea things were generally hopeful. Until now when a seed of doubt was planted in his overthinking mind.

Breaking his concentration, Tom felt a vibration in his pants making him jump. He looked around and couldn't see anyone else experiencing the sensation either. He looked down at his legs and saw a rectangular bump protruding from his left pocket. It was his phone. Before this, Tom only thought it was just another part of his body. The phone was now buzzing, and a faint glow could be see through the stitching of his khakis. Reaching into his pocket, Tom pulled the glowing object out. He quickly realized that this device is what he saw the young woman and Irene have. It was a nice distraction from the crushing crisis of existence the man next to him was having.

Was Tom's phone an Android or and iPhone? Or maybe some third option humans have yet to invent and the question of iPhone versus Android dates this book terribly. I don't know. Nor do I really care much. I'm reminded daily how attached to branding humanity is.

Humans having an attachment to a certain brand isn't in any way a negative comment. It makes sense. Just as you enjoy the company of one friend over another based on past experiences, so does one enjoy one corporation over another. I just don't think the author ever goes into it being an iPhone or Android. Maybe it's a crucial fact or maybe it's not.

Tom did have headphones connected to it though. As the phone lit up and turned on, illuminating his pudgy face, Tom touched the screen. He didn't know exactly what he was doing but was catching on quickly. He tapped on a musical icon he recognized. He didn't know why he recognized it, but it was information in his head that suddenly appeared. Curious, he tapped on the button reading "Play". A nice upbeat song started to fade into his ears. It felt happy and his heart danced with the rhythm. The album cover on the front showed a fierce woman baring a sword surrounded by two large dragons. As he listened, the woman's voice filled his ears and he really did quite enjoy this thing called music. He especially paid attention to the lyrics. He enjoyed the beats and felt inspired. But out of everything the woman sang about, one particular lyric stood out. The lyric talked about kindness. The woman sang about being kind no matter what the situation. For a moment, it felt as if she was singing directly to Tom.

Letting his mind wonder away from the questions of truth and existence, Tom looked out of the window. A large flash of light split across the tree line. He could see thousands of trees stretching into the distance. For the split-second flash of light Tom saw water collecting on the ground next to the bus as they sped by. Then, there it was. One flash of lightning was all it took for Tom to no longer see that they were in the middle of a forest. The tree line ended, and Tom saw the bus was crossing a large ominous bridge. He looked to the left of the window and saw the tree line moving slowly away as they crossed the bridge. He saw the edge of the forest drop down into a steep hole the bridge was built across. The drop was massive and disappeared into a dark abyss. It was a stark warning that existence was meant for the Community Center, and not the forest.

The bridge was not constructed very well, in

fact, it looked very old and broken. The bus rumbled more often, and Tom could feel the rattle of large bumps. He tried to hold onto his warm feeling with every new revelation, but it was becoming increasingly difficult with these introductions of an old bridge and chasm to eternal darkness. If the bridge they crossed was rickety and broken, what was the Community Center going to be like? Looking to the right of the window Tom tried to see past the rain falling around the bus. His eyes squinted, as he thought it would help his view. Surprisingly, he was starting to make out a large shape in the distance. Ahead of their bus, he saw another buses lights. Another group of people just as excited and surprised by the prospect of co-existing with each other in the Community Center.

The bus Tom saw stopped ahead of their own. He felt his bus slow to a stop behind them. A large strike of lightning lit up the sky and all the surrounding ground now covered in a muddy water. Large bellowing walls shot off in either direction from the lightnings flash. Poorly constructed concrete walls shot up miles high into the sky above them disappearing into the clouds. Tom was glad his new stranger friend was not looking out the window, it was an intimidating sight to see. Two sliding doors opened next to the bus in front of their own, the light cutting through the darkness in a brilliant white. People slowly exited and entered the large building, shielding themselves from the rain as they did.

It was Tom's buses turn now. The rain slowly let up and became a light sprinkle as their bus pulled forward. Tom found the large daunting building to be oddly beautiful after a moment of letting his fear subside. The building was very plain, even with its imperfections. After all, Tom didn't know what good architecture was. He only lived in blissful ignorance like the rest of the people on the bus. It's grey boring concrete, the florescent lights flickering helplessly at any sign of disruption, and a wide-eyed look from all the sitting passengers gave Tom a sense of what existence would be.

The doors to his bus flung open and a cold breeze flooded inside. Irene had shifted a handle forcefully and suddenly to cause the abrupt change. Most people knew exactly what they were doing as they stood up to leave the bus. This left Tom and the man sitting next to him alone. Tom didn't move only because he waited for the stranger to move before he did, and the stranger didn't want to leave in the first place. But, slowly, the man stood up and walked down the aisle of the bus toward Irene who now stood handing out the ballots to every passenger. The man clearly did not want to take the ballot and kept refusing it's offer from the woman. Tom remained seated as he didn't want to become involved in conflict on his first day.

Suddenly, in a fit of annoyance, the man snatched the ballot from Irene's hand and threw it on the floor of the bus. The bus driver stood up. This was the first time any person saw him. He towered over the man. He was so incredibly giant he had to crouch slightly as to not hit his head on the roof of the bus. As terrifying as the bus driver could have made the experience, he simply attempted to calm the man down along with Irene. Unfortunately, it was to no avail. The man was adamant he did not belong here. Tom thought he could overhear him say something to the extent of "without her". Saying this caused the man to pause. It was as if he referenced someone he never knew. He looked at the ground attempting to learn more about his life in the Community Center and meeting someone in his mind. Whoever it was, Tom saw the man was upset that she wasn't there. Irene attempted to assure him everything would be okay and there were no mistakes.

The bus driver then said something very peculiar to Tom. It was up until this point Tom thought Irene was in charge. Even if he were wrong, he assumed someone would be looking over the Community Center in charge of everything. But the bus driver contradicted quickly with a booming and conversation ending voice.

"Listen, you think I wasn't scared when I was on the bus? We know just as much as you. My job is to drive out there...," the bus driver pointed toward the forest across the bridge. "...until twenty-four people appear on my bus and I drive them back here. Her job is to hand you this pamphlet. Now get off my bus and go do what it is *you're* supposed to do," the bus driver finished and lowered his hand. The man went silent. Tom could see the man knew something he wasn't telling anyone else. Tom saw him walk off the bus with his head hanging low. He looked lost. He looked hopeless.

"Come on. You gonna give us hell like him too?" the

bus driver asked Tom who snapped back to his own existence.

"No...," Tom said with a crackling voice. "...Sorry, I mean, no." he corrected his first attempt with a sterner and more confident "no". The bus driver and Irene couldn't help but think Tom was an odd type of person as he walked to the front. He was very tall, having to bend down slightly like the bus driver. Unlike the bus driver, Tom was very lanky with very little muscle mass. Tom looked like someone you knew but never tried to get to know. He was someone you would casually say hi to in a grocery store and think about how you should at least give them a call to get to know them better. But you never do. Irene and the bus driver then saw Tom's eyes. He had very kind eyes and almost a constant smile even in situations of stress. They both knew, deep down, Tom would probably be socially eaten alive once he had a taste of the real world. This is due to his unnaturally friendly behavior and curiosity.

"Here's your ballot," Irene handed Tom the rectangular piece of thick paper. Seeing it closer he saw all the different religions and various beliefs one could mark.

"I have to fill it out now?" Tom asked quizzically. Irene rolled her eyes slightly. She was just about to respond when the bus driver interrupted as he sat down in the driver's seat again.

"Like it matters if you do. We all walk through the curtain eventually regardless," Tom heard the mumbled words of the bus driver. Irene shot him a glance disapprovingly as if he wasn't supposed to have said anything.

"You can fill it out whenever you like," Irene said looking back to Tom. Tom looked down at the small rectangular ballot. He felt as though he should just be happy with whatever his friends and family mark.

Yes, Tom has friends and family even without meeting them yet. You will meet them later. If you haven't noticed, things don't necessarily move in a linear way in this book. It takes a minute to catch on.

"Wow...," Tom whispered reading through all the different choices. Christianity was top of the list, followed by Islam, something called Atheism/Agnosticism, then Hinduism, Buddhism, and lastly there was Judaism. From there he saw many other things that made the list, but it looked as though those five were the top.

"Off you go now," Irene said putting her hand on Tom's back and leading him off the bus. Tom stepped off onto the concrete below and looked behind him through the buses open doors. Irene stared at him with her hand gripped around the handle to close the doors.

"What if I get it wrong?" Tom asked her. She looked back at the bus driver. A roar of laughter echoed between the two of them as she shut the door. This was the last time he would see Irene. The bus drifted slowly away, across the bridge, and back into the forest leaving Tom standing in the rain.

Turning around, Tom saw someone familiar. The stranger who was nervous from before stood staring at the open doors peering inside the Community Center. Inside, Tom could see people walking around visiting and enjoying what looked like different shops. Some people were seated on benches talking and some were walking around with bags. The man looked above the doors where a mantra was written in large letters. It wasn't nicely written but spray painted on in a splatter of graffiti.

"A soul is the mover of the body."

A quote Tom didn't fully understand. The man continued staring at it. Tom heard him sniff from crying and could tell that this quote was breaking him. For a moment, Tom thought about saying something to him. But he didn't share in the feelings the man had, so there was clearly nothing he could do.

As if he had no control over his own body, the man suddenly knew what he had to do. The man darted from the spot he stood, into the giant doors, and past several people who were walking. What was Tom to do? That's not me asking the question. That's you asking the question and Tom wondering what kind of man he was. Was Tom a man to ignore this stranger and walk away? Or was he the type to chase after him and try and help the man as much as he could? Or was Tom the type of man who simply was curious about new experiences? Tom was an adventurer. He darted inside the doors after the man, excited at the prospect of a new experience.

Chapter III

The Third Floor

Welcome to the Community Center! Within these walls encompasses all of existence and every person who's ever lived: past, present, or future. Interestingly enough, none of them exist concurrently and yet they all exist together. You'll understand more as you read. You want to probably continue Tom's story. Unfortunately for you, we can't dive completely into what Tom experienced in his first steps inside the Community Center yet. We can't discuss the multitude of people walking around or the various shops Tom saw. We can't discuss the dark and light feelings Tom felt looming in the center of the Community Center.

Why? That's what I love about you. Always asking questions. Always pushing forward to understand something even if I know the answer and you don't. It's a fun game we play but you continue trusting me in revealing the story exactly how it's supposed to play out. And right now, it isn't by following Tom anymore. Don't worry, he's still our main character. But shifting focus for a moment will give more cinematic and interesting events later on. I know, I know, we'll get back to Tom. I promise you the next chapter we'll pick up right where Tom left off. Well, funny because technically Tom has already passed all the things you're about to read. But that's something else you'll understand more as you continue to read.

No, right now we're going to speak about a slightly older professor. He isn't incredibly old but old enough you would assume he has a few words of wisdom to share from his experiences in the Community Center. He wears a nice jacket over a warm sweater, his shoes glisten from a shoeshine he had earlier in the day, and hair only grows on the left and right side of his head. He walks slowly through the hallways and corridors of the Community Center much farther away from any other souls who might see him. But it isn't from a need to distance himself from others but rather a want to find something in the dark crevices of the Community Center that few others had found. The book clutched in his right hand is a personal journal filled with notes and ideas scribbled out. On the small book was inscribed his first name "Clive". These are from moments in his existence when he tried to understand the Community Center on a deeper level and understand his belief known as Christianity. Who was God? Why did he create this confusing place? And, more importantly to Clive, who was Lucifer? Who was the dark shadowy creature lurking in the Community Center only to deceive the ones within?

It's something Tom doesn't know about yet, evil. Evil exists in the Community Center. Whether or not an inhabitant of the Community Center believes it or not. It is represented in some form in every story. It may take on the form of Satan, a demon, natural occurrences, or the inhabitants themselves. Evil does exist and often it is searched out to try and explain why it exists.

Clive is a Christian, so he subscribes that Lucifer is the evil lurking in the shadows. This creature, Biblically, is a fallen angel looking to lie to the Community Center and turn them away from... God? Or Christianity? That's an interesting thought. Does Clive look for an evil that wishes to turn those away from God or from Clive's religion? Thomas Lewis, as you'll find out, is a Christian also. But does he also subscribe to the belief that Satan is a winged creature perched on our shoulders attempting to sway us away from his own religion? Because if either Tom or Clive had any sense about the matter, they would understand that if Lucifer's goal was to sway them away from Christianity then God would still remain. Of course, within the narrative of Christianity. And who knows if that's the right religion or not.

I'm getting ahead of myself though. I do that sometimes but it's because I'm just so danged excited to see things unfold. And you know what? I can do that.

Clive walked through the corridors; his journal tightly clasped in his hand as he sought out the representation of evil in the Community Center. After many meetings with ones who claimed to have met evil, he knew he was only moments away from finding it. He wasn't wrong. Hidden around various corridors and passageways, the guidance given to Clive was correct. As Clive quietly walked through the division of the Community Center known as Phestiles, he found a door hidden in obvious view for everyone to see. Behind the door Clive found something that was only ever rumored in the Community Center. He found a staircase. Most on the first floor of the Community Center knew about the elevator leading to the second floor of the Community Center. But very few spoke of a staircase or even the existence of one. Those in Phestiles and the opposite division, Acedia, were prone to keep these legends only ever as legends. If it were true of a hidden staircase's existence, then it may be true that a third floor existed as well. A third floor where this dark creature lived filling the Community Center with darkness and evil.

How confusing it must be for you though. The title of this book is "Time is on the Second Floor". Not "What is on the Third Floor?" So why do I insist on following this storyline of a mysterious third floor where evil lurks? It's good story progression! That's why! Just because it doesn't look like what you're used to doesn't mean it isn't the same though. I tease some terrible evil thing in the beginning and the rest of the story builds up to the climactic ending. Introduce a tease of Thanos in the first Avengers and then follow through with an epic finale. You're welcome for a Marvel reference in a philosophical and theological fiction.

Clive opened the door and saw the harsh flores-cent lights beating down on him. His eyes looked up the concrete steps and saw where they led. He stepped forward and walked up the thirty-three steps of each staircase, eventually making it to a door that had a large number three hanging on the front. The number was golden metal screwed into a wooden door. Before Clive grasped the handle of the door, he was surprised by how shiny it was. This showed to Clive how often the door was used. Clive chuckled as he realized evil was often used even in daily life. He opened the door and walked into the large room.

Immediately the light from the staircase shifted into darkness. Surrounding the room were old chairs stacked for storage, blankets thrown over mirrors, and various objects stored away never to be seen again. Above was a large glass dome letting the view of dark clouds roaming above. Seeing the clouds so close to the Community Center was very different for Clive. If one were to stand on the outside of the Communi-ty Center, the clouds would seem thousands of miles away. But here on the third floor, the clouds were a fog surrounding the glass dome. Clive immediately knew that the third floor was a place of power over the rest of the Community Center. This was an intentional metaphor evil wanted everyone to know who entered. Evil was above everything.

In the center of the room directly under the large dome there sat a dragon. The dragon had the proportions of a man sitting behind a wooden desk. You read that correctly, it was indeed a dragon. But unlike the dragons of fairy tales and myth, this dragon sat like a man and wore a nice suit to convey authority. The table in front of him was beautifully carved and designed with perfect purpose in this place. The table was created to be in the image of an even fiercer creature which seemed almost impossible in the presence of the already terrifying dragon. The dragon had two sharp horns that were much shorter than what one would assume a dragon to have. From the dragon's scaly scalp they curled outward wonderfully.

The dragon immediately noticed Clive walking into its domain. It gave a small grin watching the human from the first floor come to visit. Clive thought his feelings about the dragon to be odd. He searched for this evil and now, as he stood in its presence, he didn't feel uncomfortable at all. In fact, Clive felt a slight excitement to see the dragon like he was in the presence of an old friend. Clive unknowingly grinned back at the beast sitting in its chair. The dragon lifted its sharp fingers and gestured for Clive to come and sit with him. Clive didn't refuse. He walked over to the extravagant table built specifically for the dragon and sat down. He placed his journal on the table and relaxed himself.

The dragon tapped lightly on the table as if it were

waiting for Clive to say something. But he said nothing. He only studied the craftsmanship of the table. Its image came together for Clive as he saw seven heads of the beast who looked fiercer than the dragon.

"It was built for me by those below," the dragon spoke. Its voice sounded exactly how a dragon would sound if one ever did speak. Crackling of fire hidden behind deep and gruff sounds washed over the air and into Clive's ears. Clive looked up from the table and into the dragon's eyes. They didn't look like what Clive expected evil's eyes to look. They were old and worn eyes who had seen many things in their lifetime. Clive quickly dismissed this thought as he was aware of the deceitful nature evil could convey. And so, he knew he would not be fooled. But does a fool ever know when he is truly being deceived?

"This table was not built by either Phestiles or Acedia. No, it was built by the complete and unified Community Center in a time to come," the dragon explained as he too looked at its craftmanship. The dragon spoke of a future where the Community Center did not quarrel over the meaning of life. But those are stories for another time.

"I suspect you know the game we play," the dragon asked as it stopped pondering the table. The question wasn't a surprise. Evil would only appear before you as a representation of itself. Your intention must always be to play its game. Just as they sat there, Clive remembered when he was told about the game from someone who had met evil long ago.

"I don't know if it will come to you in the form it took with me. A beautiful woman laced with fine silk. But I knew it was the beast itself. I knew it was evil. It will look you in the eyes. Absolute evil. But you will think and feel welcome and as if all your questions have been answered. But there's a catch as there always is with evil. To rid the world of it's evil, you must tell the evil what exactly what it represents. If you are right, then you will be given the chance to debate the evil. If you win then it will relinquish its power unto you. And the evil will be no more." Clive remembered the man telling him before.

The dragon continued staring at Clive waiting for his answer. He nodded his head. Leaning forward, Clive flipped open his journal and read his notes. The dragon continued to grin.

"You..." Clive stuttered slightly. The dragon cackled as Clive coughed to reassure his own perceived authority.

"You are apathy," Clive told the dragon. He'd thought about this for a long time. What exactly the great evil of the Community Center represented. What is the commonality between all evils making it the greatest more than anything else? For Clive, it was apathy. It made sense if you thought about it.

The dragon smiled gritting its sharp teeth. This was the only moment Clive felt a sense of fear rather than comfort. If he were wrong, then the dragon would cast him out and he would never have the chance to come back. If he were right, then he would be in for a debate on why apathy is needed for the Community Center to exist or not. Ultimately giving Clive the chance to banish evil from all of existence.

"You are right," the dragon finally said to Clive. A wave of relief emptied itself but was immediately followed by a terrible realization that Clive would now have the chance to save the Community Center from evil.

"So where would you like to begin? Why do you think apathy shouldn't exist in the Community Center? Do you think people shouldn't be given the choice between apathy and passion? Maybe you think people shouldn't have free will at all?" the dragon spat out in full force. Clive quickly rummaged through his notes looking for answers to the philosophical questions. Quickly he pointed at a note.

"It's not whether or not apathy should exist in the Community Center, it's whether or not you should be swaying people to be apathetic rather than passionate," Clive shot back with his argument quickly. The dragon didn't sway. In fact, it looked as though his argument only strengthened the dragon.

"I'm only a concept and as a concept shouldn't I have the right to expand people's minds to new ideas? Even if those ideas are a lack of caring, maybe in the end... that is the answer. Afterall, every religion gets its say in swaying people to any different belief. The ballot is full of ideas any person can vote on. How am I any different from a new religion?" the dragon replied. Clive noticed the dragon was speaking as though he'd had this argument many times before. As if those who came before him guessed apathy as well. The dragon had won this argument countless times.

Clive slowly closed his journal and leaned back in his chair. Knowing the dragon had already defeated countless others with the same arguments crushing Clive. The dragon leaned back as well mimicking him. Studying the dragon, Clive knew this was an empty argument where he would find no answers. Somehow, Clive knew he had already lost the debate.

"You've had this debate before," he told the dragon now looking disappointed.

"Awe, I will admit you are slightly cleverer than those before you. Normally I get in a few more arguments before casting them out from my domain," the dragon breathed out in reply. Clive, feeling foolish, stood up from the table and picked up his journal.

"No need to cast me out. I will leave on my own accord," he said as he began walk away.

"You can see why I am the top of the Community Center. Even the curtain is below me. Everything is below me. I am and always will be," the dragon spat out as Clive exited the dusty old room beneath the clouds.

Frankly, I think the dragon was a bit rude at the end. No need to kick a man while he's down. Clive believed he knew the greatest evil to plague humanity. He only realized while speaking with it that every other person also thought the same thing. Apathy, or some form of evil still reigned supreme in the Community Center.

Chapter IV

Green Grass and Dark Fabric

Tom stopped mid-run between two corners and a hallway leading towards a large opening in the Community Center. Blinding white light filled the opening with the silhouette of the man Tom followed. Tom assumed the man stopped to catch his breath. The man was very quick after all. Tom wondered if there was an inhuman element to the man or if all people in the Community Center were naturally this fast. This would mean Tom was very slow in comparison. Along with being very fast, Tom noticed the strange way the man was able to weave in and out of the people who wandered the hallways. Tom understood he should probably be familiarizing himself with the Community Center and all its people, but he felt a sense of duty to calm the man down. The mystery of this man was intriguing to Tom and if he could put his mind at ease, then it was something he would do his best to help with.

As the two men ran, Tom's curiosity kept rising as he noticed that none of the people seemed to care about the man running. They did, however, get quite annoyed with Tom continuously bumping into them. It was as if they had seen the running man so many times before they didn't mind him at all.

Tom's mind ran wild as he past various shops, markets, and gatherings of people. Everything looked like a well-oiled machine for people to exist, only being disrupted by at least one man (Tom) running into everyone. The man Tom followed was amazing. It was graceful to watch his back arch and legs twist to move past different people. The only thing missing was the music to his elusive dance. He never touched a single person and none of the people moved out of his way or seemed to change their course at all. Tom was not as successful. He thought to himself that bumping into everyone was a terrible first impression to give the people of the Community Center. But he didn't care. Tom didn't ask why he didn't care. He simply had a calling to this stranger who needed help.

Now Tom was stopped between two corners watching the man stand in the silhouette of light. The hall in front of him was not as discolored as the rest of the Community Center. It had a bright red carpet stretched in the middle. Graffiti lined both walls leading to the opening at the end. Quotes of comfort and love made Tom feel very nice about existence. There were thousands of pictures tacked to the ceiling. Pictures of people with friends and family smiling and having a good time. It was a beautiful scenery to behold. Tom wondered if the man even noticed the decorative hallway. More importantly, Tom wondered where the hallway led. What was behind the sheet of white light illuminating the hallway brilliantly?

Tom sighed as he regained his breath. There were no other people in the beautiful hallway. Only Tom and the stranger stood looking forward. And suddenly, it was just Tom. The man stepped forward, swallowed by the sheet of white light. Tom stepped into the hallway. He didn't look at the quotes or the pictures hanging above him. He only wanted to know where the man went. There was a connection to this stranger he didn't know. There was a mysterious desire to understand him Tom wanted to seek out.

He stepped onto the threshold of the white sheet and it's haze disappeared. He could see the room where the man stepped into. It was much larger than he thought it would be. It was an enormous circular park in the middle of the Community Center. Several other entrances could be seen on other parts of the wall leading to this park. Bright green grass covered the park and filled the air with it's scent. Large trees cast long shadows to the outward walls as a bright light shined downward on the park. It was a place filled with beautiful life and warmth. It was stunning to Tom, such a magnificent area in the middle of a much more mundane building. It reminded him of the large hole surrounding the Community Center. Wonderous hills of grass bounded up and down around the park until you reached the middle. In the center of the park where the grass flattened again into a small field. Following the grass to the center, Tom could see the man walking towards a large object standing in the middle of the field.

The structure in the center of the park held no place of comfort for Tom when his eyes saw it. He saw no joy or love being poured from that place. Tom would like to label the sensation he felt as ominous or terrifying. Maybe it was how he was supposed to view what he saw, but he only felt ignorant to what it meant. A curtain draped over a circular object hung in the middle of the park. This curtain was at least twenty-feet high; the curtain fell to the grass below just barely touching the fields blades. It's black emptiness of color almost consumed the colorful grass surrounding it. The long curtain hid any sign of what was behind it. The Community Center and the park all pointed to its encompassing aura penetrating anyone who looked at it. In an odd way, Tom thought it was beautifully contrasted against everything else he saw. It almost made everything else in the park that much more colorful because of its mysterious flow.

The curtain suddenly moved but from any breeze or wind in the park. Tom saw a person from another entrance grasp it's dark fabric, lifted it up, and walked on the other side. Looking around he saw more people walking towards the curtain. Each at a time, each person lifted the curtain and walked behind it. Like bugs drawn to a light, they trapped themselves behind it. Surrounding the area in the park there were people having nice picnics on the hills. Some people were wailing in sadness. Some people laughed, but not at the people walking towards the curtains. They were laughing together to keep their tears from coming. Tom didn't know how to react. He didn't know what this place was or what it was for. The people would vanish behind the curtain and soon there would be no more room inside the circle. But they must have vanished because more people came without anyone exiting the curtain. People would enter the curtain but never come back.

Tom then saw the stranger he met on the bus walking up to the curtain. The man looked at it for a long moment and Tom continued to watch. Something in Tom's heart was calling out towards the stranger but he felt frozen in place. He could only stare on as the man touched the fabric. As the man's palm traced it's fabric, he suddenly grasped it in his hand. Alone, the man lifted the curtain into the unknown. He stepped inside and the curtain gently fell back into place. Tom's breath was taken away. A tear rolled down his eye as he watched this man walk behind the curtain. Something wasn't right, something was very wrong, but Tom had no idea what it was. He barely had a concept of what "wrong" actually meant and now he was making judgements on an existence he was unwillingly a part of. Within an instance, Tom knew the man was gone forever. He knew he would never see him again, and his heart cried out.

Touching the side of the entrance he stood, Tom grasped his chest feeling it beat faster. He didn't understand what happened but could tell it was much bigger than him. The circular curtain could not have been more than seven feet in diameter. These people were not returning from the curtain. He looked around at the people having picnics. Some enjoying themselves and some were crying. But Tom felt something else standing amid the curtain. Fear cast a shadow over Tom's mind that day. Fear of the unknown was something he never anticipated, and now he was standing in its presence.

"David!" a woman shrieked. Tom jumped at the high-pitched sound of her voice. He looked to his right and saw a woman on her knees crying out. Her face was covered by the palms of her hands as she rocked back and forth. Tom looked back to the curtain and then back to her. She slowly lifted her head from her hands.

"He's gone. I can't believe he's gone," she whispered into the warm air of the park. Tom instinctively could see this woman knew the stranger who walked through the curtain. She turned her head slowly to look at Tom. He was in shock from the curtain and the screaming of the strange woman.

"You... you could have saved him!" she screamed at Tom who fell against the wall from her outburst. Staring at him she kept repeating that Tom could have saved him from something. He didn't know how to react, he kept backing away down the hall as she remained on her knees crying out. Tom felt the whirlwind of questioning in his mind but now the emotions he once loved to experience were running rampant. Fear, sadness, and anger were building up inside him. His heart pounded quicker and sweat started pouring down his skin.

Everything slowed down for Tom. He stumbled down the hallway, his vision blurred, he could only make out the red carpet to exit the hallway. He stepped back into the Community Centers normal concrete floor trying to fix his head. Oddly enough, Tom's thoughts were practically normal. But his brain was experiencing an anxiety attack. He knew he needed to relax before he passed out. He tried to think of any answers during his time on the bus, but he thought he must have missed something Irene told them. Walking through the hallways in the Community Center, no one seemed to mind that he was having a panic attack. People went about their daily business like normal paying no attention to him. He passed men and women as they walked back and forth between places. Occasionally he overheard someone mention that he "was the man bumping into everyone earlier." Hundreds of people going about their lives. He moved through the crowds slowly, his vision going in and out, until he couldn't stand.

He felt the breeze of air hit his face as he fell to the ground but didn't feel the impact. He felt his head swing forward as his body was caught by someone. Spit exited his mouth and splashed on the ground. A man stood him back up.

"Go about your day everyone. Just a fellow person in need," the new stranger said looking around at all the people. Tom could see the man through his blurred vision but could see he was shorter than Tom.

"Hey, you alright? What's going on? You need medicine or something?" the man asked Tom whose heartbeat was now relaxing. Tom still felt like a zombie amongst everyone else. Tom's eyes slowly shut, and he felt his weight being lifted. His eyes opened slightly again, and he saw the front doors to the Community Center slide open as he was taken outside. He was still standing but only barely. His feet slid across the floor with each step as the man helped him along. He smelled the damp concrete, the green woods in the distance, and felt the small sprinkle of rain against his face as he was placed on his feet again. He thought of the woman from the bus, the beautiful girl who looked embarrassed to be caught staring at him. He didn't get to catch her before she left and wondered if he would ever see her again.

Opening his eyes, he looked closely at the trees far off in the distance over the large hole surrounding the Community Center. It was the forest he came from. He took a deep breath feeling much better from when he was in the cramped spaces inside. Taking another deep breath, his lungs were filled with a stench unknown to him. It wasn't an absolute horrid smell but gave Tom's nose discomfort. He scrunched up his nose and turned his head to his right to see who the culprit was.

"You really gave me a little bit of a scare," the man who saved him said. A cigarette hung loosely between his lips as he too looked at the far away forest line. The man was shorter than Tom but not by much. He was bald with a twelve-a-clock shadow covering his mouth and jaw. He wore a nice shirt with a logo Tom didn't recognize and blue jeans. He didn't look like much but was nice enough to carry Tom outside for fresh air. "Acedia isn't known for wanting to help others. If it interferes with them, then they'll stop. Other than that, don't expect much," the man said.

"Yeah... um... thanks," Tom replied under his breath turning to look at the forest again. The man rocked himself back and forth on his heels to become more comfortable and familiar with his space. Smoke entered his lungs and exited into the quiet night air. Confused, Tom put his hands in his pockets to help his subconscious with the awkward silence.

"Still don't know who I am?" the stranger asked Tom. This was a weird question. Tom only existed for maybe an hour; he hadn't met anyone yet. But the man already assumed they knew each other. "Give it a few minutes. It'll kick in," the man said with a smug look on his face. Tom couldn't reply. His thoughts were recollecting the events he witnessed upon entering the Community Center.

"His name was David," Tom whispered under his breath. He realized the woman was yelling the name of the man he followed.

"What? My names not David," the man who saved Tom said almost offended. He stopped rocking back and forth and took his cigarette out of his mouth, now unsure what would happen next.

"No, not you. Somebody else," Tom said, still in a whispering tone. The man next to him stuck the cigarette back in his mouth as Tom still slowly comprehended what happened. Looking to his right again he saw Eric was putting out his cigarette on his shoe.

This almost caused another anxiety attack for Tom. He suddenly knew the man standing next to him. He realized the man's name was Eric Clay. Tom's eyes widened staring at the stranger slowly turning into a recognized face in his mind. Eric was a person he'd spent a large part of his existence with. The two were very close friends most of their existence. Tom was flooded with knowledge about Eric. He'd met Eric's parents and entire family, they often argued about politics and different movies they liked.

Eric's face split a grin across his face as he continued to look at the forest. He could tell Tom was beginning to recognize him. "Feels weird doesn't it? Recognizing someone you've never met," Eric said looking at Tom. There was a dazed expression to Tom as Eric continued staring at him. Tom's mouth could barely move. "Don't worry man, the first night is always the hardest. You're still getting used to things," Eric said comforting him.

"This is a lot," Tom finally spat out. Eric laughed a

little.

"Yeah, I remember when I first recognized you. Same thing happened to me." Although this reply from Eric was odd, Tom was too preoccupied with *knowing* someone he'd never met to register what he said. "Listen, existence is weird. That should be the first thing they tell you on the bus. They don't tell us much in general anyway. Besides the curtain, it's...."

"What about the curtain?" Tom asked cutting Eric off. He accepted the quick knowledge of suddenly knowing someone and having memories with that person, but the curtain still remained a mystery to Tom. Eric looked at him confused.

"What do you mean?" Eric asked. Tom didn't know what to say. He thought his question was pretty clear. "You really don't know about the curtain?" Eric asked him. Tom shook his head as if it were obvious he wouldn't know.

"I don't know what to tell you man. The curtain is pretty common knowledge. At some point during your existence, you'll drop whatever you're doing, and walk to the curtain. You'll go behind it and never come back," Eric explained to him. Tom felt even worse than before as his fear of David's outcome became a reality. He would never see David again.

"You're a weird dude, you know that? You've always been weird, but I didn't know we'd meet again like this," Eric continued. He was not attempting to insult Tom and Tom didn't register it that way. Wrapped up in the thoughts of not knowing a key piece of information from the Community Center, Tom was being thrown further down the rabbit hole David was cast in.

"Here, what's your belief?" Eric asked hoping it would break the tension of questions plastered on Tom's face.

"What?" Tom replied, trying to figure out what Eric meant by "belief".

"The back of your card... here," he said grabbing the ballot out of Tom's front pocket and flipping it over. "...on the back of everyone's ballot is the belief they start out with. It's usually what your parents will have too," Eric explained to him. But Tom couldn't understand how they knew each other well enough to be best friends but didn't know each other's beliefs.

Tom looked back to see the tree line. He felt a little bit more comfortable looking at them. Sure, they all looked the same, but they were all unique and different in subtle ways. If the forest was where he came from then maybe there was something to going back where it all began like David originally proposed. Instead of ending in the curtain with uncertainty, maybe going back would be the answer.

"There, you're a Christian...," Eric said putting the ballot back into Tom's front pocket. Eric walked out near the edge of the hole and looked down inside. It stretched far into the darkness. "...not a surprise. Martha and Albert are very Christian," Eric said. Tom walked over to Eric and put his hand on his back, accepting the things he was being shown.

"Thank you, Eric," he told him with a grin.

"Of course, I'm glad you're back. I've been bored," Eric said, which confused Tom, but he knew knowledge would be something non-linear. Tom, Eric, and everyone's existence was all over the place. The two men turned around and headed back into the Community Center.

"Who are Martha and Albert?" Tom asked quizzically as they walked. Eric paused and smiled.

"They're your parents," he said. Tom smiled and the doors to the Community Center shut as they walked inside.

Chapter V

Chicken Fingers

Thomas Lewis was a Christian... *is* a Christian. I don't know if he still subscribed to that belief or not. But in this chapter of the story, it's at least what his ballot said. Now, Tom being a Christian is an interesting conundrum in of itself. Being a Christian is interesting but it's something I need to reiterate because we often forget there are several different types of Christianity. I promise, we'll get back to the story in a moment.

In the Community Center there is an overall view of what a Christian is, and then there are many different denominations sprouting off from the central Christian faith. These denominations separate people from what the core of being a "Christian" is. Like a tree with many branches springing from the same trunk, Christianity also grows many branches from it's trunk.

A Christian can hold multitudes of different beliefs all branching from the same core idea. The core ideology is "Jesus Christ is God, he died for humanities sins, and came back as the savior of humanity." If all Christians believe this fundamental steppingstone then why are there so many varieties of the belief? Take the Catholic denomination. They consider themselves to be the first denomination of the Christian faith. They wouldn't even consider themselves a denomination, they would consider themselves "The Church". The difference between them and more popularized Western teachings is they believe in Jesus's salvation and good works to get into heaven.

See, now I'm moving ahead of myself. Heaven is a belief on the ballot outside the belief of Christianity. The belief of an afterlife paradise is like any other belief. It's the idea that once a person moves beyond the curtain, they obtain paradise for eternity. This is usually based on how one lived in existence. The small amount of time living in existence, determines exactly how you will live in eternity. A funny thing to imagine, considering humanity can't even understand what eternity is in the first place. It's easy to throw the word "eternity" around when no one has ever experienced it. Along this same belief in the eternal paradise, if you don't do well in your small time of existence, then you are sent to hell. This is where you burn for eternity (in the broadest sense possible).

To understand this concept is to understand Tom's beginning confusion with existence. Tom's category of "Christian" was of "Non-denominational". This was a sort of church who found religious practices to be boring and outdated. They wished to modernize the old teachings and show Christianity was more about relationship than it was about religion. Their belief was the close relationship individuals held with Jesus, rather than a God and servant dynamic. With this belief, Christians also hold that Jesus was the only one to wipe your sins clean. Obtaining eternal paradise (heaven) could only be obtained through him.

Staring at the ballot felt silly and restrictive to Tom. The words written inside its pages didn't force Tom to believe in anything but only lay out what the people in the Community Center grasped onto for understanding. Flipping the ballot, he could see many boxes were unchecked. He could choose anything he wanted from his original Christian answer. He could be a Buddhist and believe internal peace was the way to break the bondage of existence. Ultimately still ending in eternal paradise. He could be something involving New Age. Tom could see many similarities between Buddhism and New Age. They both had a belief rooted in internal peace. But he would want to speak with someone who believed in either before making such a stark assumption. Tom could believe in fact and what we can see by marking down science for his belief. After all, who was he to argue with scientists who have spent their entire existence proving the Community Center was all there was to existence. Every belief ever conceived was printed on the pages of the ballot. Every single one designed in one form or another to explain why Tom existed and where David disappeared to beyond the curtain.

This forced Tom to think a little heavier on the matter. David knew. David saw the existence he occupied space in, he understood everything Tom understood, and yet, David understood one other thing right now. David knew what was beyond the curtain. There was something just beyond the curtain prodding at Tom's mind. He didn't understand why his heart cried out when a complete stranger stepped beyond it but didn't understand what was keeping him from walking through it just to see what happened. One reason was Tom knew he would never be able to return if he did walk through it. He would have wasted his existence. But maybe existence wasn't important anyway? Maybe walking through the curtain as if it meant nothing was the answer to being able to come back from it.

Tom wanted to experience existence. He wanted to see what it was before moving to the next experience. But he also knew he couldn't just blindly follow the words written on the ballot. Humanity constantly tries to answer how to live in existence only to try and prove ourselves worthy of something after the curtain. Tom didn't think anyone had any better idea than anyone else though. This was a humbling thought.

"What are your beliefs? About the curtain I mean," Tom asked Eric as they walked looking at large food shops. The shops looked similar to the ones you would see in a mall. But the difference was the freshness of the food they carried. Every hallway separating sections was a block similar to a city block. And within these blocks were people who lived and grew their own types of foods and goods for the Community Center to shop. This was how Acedia found it's peace in the mutual transactions of its citizens.

As the two men walked, Tom knew Eric was searching for something to eat, although Tom had never eaten anything himself. Eric, ignoring Tom's question, meandered to his left and found a small shop built into the side of the Community Center where chicken and potato fries were sold. Tom was curious, he knew what food was, but didn't understand why there were so many different types of food. Food was merely fuel for the body to keep it running. Tom stood next to Eric in the line behind a woman whose hair was bright blonde and looked like the poster child for a mid-western family.

"Of course you mean the curtain. It's the only thing you could mean when you're talking about belief," Eric said sarcastically. Unknown to Eric but the woman directly in front of him was overhearing the conversation. Tom thought about Eric's statement. It was the understanding by Eric that beliefs were solely about what was after the curtain. The beginning only pointed toward the end.

"It's not all about the curtain," the woman said turning around to face the two men. Eric sighed, knowing this would lead to unneeded conflict about beliefs. Tom didn't know why this annoyed Eric. It seemed the woman had something she could offer the conversation.

"Please, enlighten us as you wait for your chicken tenders like the rest of us," Eric told her. Her face took offence by the attitude in his voice. She quickly wiped her emotion away looking only at Tom.

"Existence has many wonderful things. Don't walk around sulking in the idea that one day you'll go through the curtain...," she said. No matter how much Eric was annoyed by the woman, this statement made Tom feel a little better. "...even if all you do *is* experience chicken tenders. Then experience them fully," she finished looking back to Eric. Tom looked back to him. Eric didn't seem to be phased by what she said. Eric look back and motioned the woman to exit stage right with both his arms. She huffed at his rude gesture and walked away.

Tom followed her with his eyes. She walked to a small table to wait for her food and he wondered what she believed. What were the steps she took to make her think the way she did? How was she so certain in what she said? For that matter, how was anyone ever so certain with their beliefs? He turned back to see Eric now finishing up his order. Eric gestured for Tom to step forward and order. Instead, Tom assumed the conversation was still on beliefs and that the young woman behind the counter was now a part of that conversation.

"Hi! I'm a Christian. What do you think happens after the curtain?" Tom asked with a large smile putting his hand out in greeting. The young woman behind the counter didn't know how to react to his odd demeanor. Tom had a strange comfortability with the curtain which would be off-putting to most people.

"You'll have to forgive my friend. He's new, and by new, I mean he is much newer than I realized. He'll have the same thing as me. Thank you," Eric cut in explaining to the woman. She could only shake her head as she put in her order. Tom, smiling still, gave the young woman a wave as Eric pulled on his shirt to follow him.

The two sat down at a small table situated around the chicken shop. People moved freely around the large food court area. Some were seated and eating just as they were about to. He saw some people carrying crates of green vegetables and some were haggling over prices. Tom saw the woman from before now receiving her order. He pondered more about what she meant by enjoying existence. Was it possible the idea of existence was purely to ignore the curtain and enjoy it while it lasted? If that were true, then why not do whatever you want? *Snap snap.*

Eric snapped his fingers in front of Tom who was lost in thought. "Hey! Are you okay? I know this isn't your first time here. But you've never acted like this before. Am I the first person you've spoken to?" he asked Tom who was now returning to the conversation.

"Well, I'm only about an hour old. Why were you so dismissive of that woman before?" Tom asked him. Eric coughed loudly at hearing Tom had existed for only an hour.

"Wow. I did not know you were so young. That explains why you didn't know your parents yet. Your mom is going to be so mad your first bite of Community Center food is chicken tenders," Eric said ignoring Tom's question. He leaned in close to Tom over the small table. "Am I the first person you've spoken to?" he asked quietly.

Tom leaned in matching Eric's secrecy, not understanding why they were whispering. "Yes, I mean, except for the guy on the bus, David," Tom said. Eric leaned back in his chair realizing there was no reason to be whispering other than dramatic effect.

"Why did he stand out to you?" Eric asked him. Tom saw the question was asked as if Tom was supposed to have a specific answer for why someone would stand out to him.

"Does it matter?" Tom quickly asked not understanding he came off as rude. Eric forgave his social mishaps, knowing he was new.

"Tom, nothing in the Community Center happens by chance. There was a reason this person stood out to you," Eric answered with brisk confidence. Tom smiled slightly hearing this. Seeing David wasn't something that happened by chance. The girl grinning at Tom on the bus didn't happen for no apparent reason. The woman who yelled at Tom that he could have saved him... didn't happen by chance.

"He was scared. No, he was terrified. Terrified is the better word...," Tom said as his tone of voice darkened.

"...he didn't want to come to the Community Center. I didn't understand why, and I never asked. I just told him everything would be okay," Tom continued. Eric could see this was leading to something darker than he anticipated. "...when we got off the bus, he ran directly for the center. That's where I saw the hallway full of pictures. That's where I saw the curtain. That's where I never saw David again," Tom finished telling Eric. He decided to leave out the part where the woman yelled at him. He was scared this was somehow his own fault in the end.

"You saw a suicide," Eric said abruptly. The word echoed into Tom's mind as he heard it spoken. "No wonder I found you almost passed out. You were close to the entrance to the park, but I didn't think you were actually there. You've been acting so strange and I never considered something like this could have happened. I'm so sorry Tom," Eric told him. The word suicide caught Tom's ears. He'd never heard it and had no knowledge of it.

A plastic tray of chicken tenders cracked on the table in front of them. The woman who took their order asked Eric if they needed anything else. Eric shook his head no, and Tom didn't notice her at all. He was only intrigued by the new word and all the experiences he was having so far keeping his focus inward.

"You don't know what suicide is. How could you? You didn't even know what the curtain was...," Eric said as he bit into a piece of chicken looking at Tom. "It's difficult to explain. The actual act is basically just deciding to go through the curtain on your own choice. Why? It comes down to the individual. Some people do it because they think there's no other way. Some people do it because they suffer from depression which leads them to suicide. There's a lot of reasons why people do it. This... David guy you met. Sounds like he didn't know how to handle... well all of this," Eric said gesturing to the Community Center around them with the wave of a piece of chicken. Tom didn't enjoy what he was hearing. He thought about his existence in the Community Center and if he should follow the example of the man he met on the bus. So far, Tom's experience with existence wasn't amazing. Suffering a panic attack and witnessing what Eric seemed to think was a great horror didn't constitute to Tom as anything particularly *good*.

"What's your belief?" Tom asked Eric whose mouth was now full of food. As he chewed on the chicken, ready to answer but unable to, Tom thought about how his friend held many interesting tidbits about existence.

"I'm an atheist," Eric said swallowing his food. "Well, I started as Church of Christ. Then, after a while, I changed my vote to atheist," Eric said as he stood up from his table. "I need a drink. You want anything?" he asked Tom who Eric could see was thinking about the word "atheist". The silence was obvious to Eric who could see Tom was struggling with all the new information. "I'll just get you what I get," Eric said leaving the table for a few moments.

Tom quickly grabbed the ballot out of his pocket

and scanned its contents. He scanned the document for the word “atheist”. There it was, typed out in the same font as all other beliefs, there sat the word “ATHEIST” written plainly with a small empty box Tom could easily mark. A small dash next to the word pointed to a short description of what it meant.

“Disbelief or lack of belief in the existence of god or gods.”

Tom sat the ballot on the table, still misunderstanding what it really meant. Unable to understand what the ballot meant by “god or gods”; Tom was unable to see what “lack of belief” meant. Although, he did notice atheism was one of the few beliefs defined by its lack of belief rather than what it believed in.

Eric returned to the table with their drinks and sat them down. Taking a drink, Eric sat in his seat. “Well? Go ahead. Ask,” he told Tom expecting him to begin with judgement for his atheism. But Tom leaned back in his chair staring at the ballot on the table.

“What is god?” Tom finally asked after a moment. He felt almost embarrassed by his ignorance. Eric took another drink from his cup, almost surprised by the question.

“I have to say. I've never met you so interested and intrigued by beliefs. Usually we would already be talking about Kate or your parents,” Eric said laughing. This was true in Tom's mind. He remembered talking to Eric about social problems or things going on in his life many times. But this time Tom felt different, he could only think about the curtain and the prospect of belief. Tom continued staring at the mysterious ballot on the table.

"You're a Christian. So you believe God created the Community Center, you believe he loves us all individually, and you believe when you go beyond the curtain you'll be in heaven because you believed in God," Eric told him hoping to put an end to the question. Eric wasn't a theologian or someone having any more answers than the next person. He was someone who lived his life quietly who wanted to leave the Community Center better than when he came.

"Okay, so I believe in God. But what is God?" Tom asked again. Eric sighed as he picked at fries on the tray. Thinking for a few minutes, he picked up a fry and put it in his mouth beginning to chew.

"You really need to talk to your mom about this. She'd know more than I would. All you need to know is that I don't believe in God. I believe in nothing at all," he told Tom who was clearly not satisfied by the answer.

"That sounds depressing. We're all just here and then we're gone. What's the point? Why don't we just do whatever we want if that's true?" Tom asked. Eric smiled. Tom could see on Eric's face he had been asked this question before. Eric was asked multiple times by many people when he changed his vote about his belief in nothing. Tom himself asked the question once but Eric didn't mind because Tom asked out of genuine curiosity. He had no leading question to try and convert him to believing in God.

"I grew up Christian. And I don't care what denomination you are or whatever spin you put on Christianity, you're a good person because you fear what might happen to you after the curtain. The problem is... being a good person out of fear doesn't make you a good person. In fact, it makes you very selfish. Atheists genuinely want to be good for the sake of being good. We don't dis-believe out of some fear of what might happen to us after the curtain. Why? Because this is all we have and if we don't have this, then we have nothing. I'd rather have this than nothing at all," Eric continued explaining more in depth why atheism isn't a depressing belief. Tom understood but didn't quite make the connection for himself. At least not enough for him to change his own vote. Tom wanted to talk to his mother about God before making the bold choice to change his vote.

"What about what's after the curtain? What's after that?" Tom asked quizzically.

"Nothing. What I just said. This is it. That's why you should be a good person. Because there is nothing after the curtain and this is all there is," Eric answered, slightly confused. Tom wasn't buying into it. Not because he had some internal warm feeling from a higher being that there had to be something after the curtain, but because it's something Eric couldn't *know*. If it were true everyone walks through the curtain, and nobody comes back, then there was no way to know if there was a God afterwards. Equally there was no way of knowing if there was nothing afterwards.

"What is nothing?" Tom asked Eric who sighed

again.

"Is this our whole friendship now? Just constant talk about the ballot and beliefs?" Eric asked frustrated. They both sat in silence not knowing where to go from there. Eric spent a lot of his existence telling people there was nothing after the curtain.

"The absence of all this. It's the absence of your consciousness. You're not there because you no longer exist. I don't know how to explain it because it's impossible to explain. I exist, I can't describe what it's like without me. We can't really think the concept of nothing," Eric explained. Tom (of course) didn't care for this answer. This only made Tom question more.

"Then how do you know all of this isn't nothing?" Tom asked. Eric held his head and put his elbow on the table.

"Because Tom, this exists. We live and we breathe. I'm conscious and you're conscious," Eric said.

"Does it? You said yourself, the concept of nothing is impossible to explain. It's impossible to even think. So how do we know this isn't nothing? What if existence is nothing? That would make the curtain nothing. Tom was snowballing as Eric saw all of the thoughts begin to collect and spit out.

"You can't just say that this is nothing Tom. It clearly is something," Eric sighed again rubbing his temple.

"But how? How can you prove to me that any of this is real?" Tom asked, unphased by the weight of the conversation he was purporting.

"It can be both ways Tom. Sure, prove all day that

none of this exists. But something exists. Whether all of this is fake, and it turns out to be a big game show set up by aliens, or all of this is a stage for a movie in another dimension, we don't know. But what we do know is that this isn't nothing and that something exists," Eric said. Tom looked at him almost with a gleam in his eye resting in a friendly grin. Eric took notice to this and realized the contradiction he had made himself.

"No! Just because something exists here doesn't mean nothing isn't after the curtain! We just don't know what's after the curtain!" Eric smiled arguing back to Tom. There was a certain respect to one another as they argued over their beliefs.

"That's my whole point! Neither of us know!" Tom laughed as he picked up the ballot and waved it around. "It's anyone's best guess really!" Tom exclaimed. Eric's laughs vanished into pondering what Tom said. It was very interesting to hear it explained this way. He was hearing that the curtain is a mystery just like exploring new territories. Tom was thinking of the curtain as practically as he could.

"Eat your chicken," Eric told him putting an end to the conversation. Tom's laugh slowly disappeared as he looked down at the food he hadn't touched. It was just food to Tom, nothing special.

"I don't really need to eat right now," Tom told his good friend.

"I didn't ask if you needed to eat. You want to know something exists? Eat the chicken," he smiled at Tom.

Three chicken fingers, fries on the side, and a

little cup of gravy sat on his side of the plastic tray. Surely, whatever this was, wasn't enough proof for their conversation about nothing and existence. Tom had never eaten before. He only knew it was to keep his body going. It was fuel to burn. Regardless, Tom picked up a piece of the crispy chicken, dipped one end in the gravy as he saw Eric do earlier, and held it close to his mouth. He opened his mouth letting his lips apart and bit into the chicken. Immediately the gravy melted on his tongue. It moved around his teeth in a beautiful, synchronized dance. The chickens crunchy outer shell leapt up and down between his top and bottom teeth as Tom tasted food for the first time. It's succulent juiciness was a delightful surprise to Tom. He closed his eyes and simply enjoyed the meal in front of him. Surely, this was reason enough to not go through the curtain. Tom thought about how Eric was showing him how to exist if only for the chicken in front of him. He thought about the woman standing in line who frustrated Tom. And he thought about how odd it was for Eric and the woman to disagree with each other, but at the same time seemed to have the same belief.

"Just wait. This is only the food they cook in the hallways. Your mom is an amazing cook," Eric said.

Chapter VI

A Puzzling Encounter

I'll bet you forgot about me. The thing inside your brain listening to you read the story of Thomas Lewis. Remember? I haven't left, not yet anyway. Could I leave? That's an interesting thought. If I left your brain and no one was around to listen to your thoughts, would you still be able to think at all? Or would your thoughts echo between the walls of your skull until they disappeared into nothingness.

Nothingness, that's a joke. We heard Tom and Eric talk about the concept of nothingness. Tom seems to think it's entirely possible for the Community Center to actually *be* nothing. I have my doubts though. Not that it isn't impossible to think "something" could be "nothing". But Tom and Eric weren't arguing over fact. They only argued about different possibilities. To define "nothing" as the absence of "something" is to assume there are only two default distinctions of "reality" or "something". Simply put, there is either "something" or there is "nothing". To question this sounds almost juvenile. Asking a question like this has no foundation to the claim. But maybe we need a little bit more of juvenile wonder in existence.

There is no evidence to prove "something" can simply be outside of existence and outside of "nothing". Because just by describing "something" forces it to fall into the category of existence. If "something" *is*... then it exists. If "something" *isn't*... then it does not exist. That tracks simply enough. But if existence cannot come from "nothing", then how did that existence come to be? It didn't come from nothing. And from what we observe, everything has a cause and effect. Maybe not in the Community Center where time is still debated greatly. But the existence of the Community Center could not have come from "nothing". So, if we know existence is real, then "something" must be outside of existence to set it into motion.

I've had these questions in my head before and after today. Because before you picked up this book they existed on the pages. After you set this book down... they will still be held within these pages. You've also had these questions in some form in your life. Some of you have chosen to ignore the deep end and some of you dip your toe in just to see how the water feels. Everyone questions what is after the curtain and their place in the cosmos of existence. That is a normal question to ask. But the question we seem to turn our heads from and keep in the recesses of our mind, so deep that the only thing who knows where to find it is the only thing that's ever heard it.

The question, what then? Let's say, for example, an omnipotent God lives outside the "something" or "nothing" conundrum. This God broke through the sky right now and floated towards the surface giving us an absolute truth for who we are and what purpose we serve. No matter your religion, this event happens, and we are bestowed with an absolute and objective truth. But what would day forty-two look like? For that matter, what would the next several years look like? What would we be doing? What would be the new standard of normal in this new truth? If paradise is everything I've ever wanted and more, what happens after? What happens when I eat the promised cake at the end of life and am left with an empty plate? It's a disturbing question you've had at least once in your life. Humanity talks about eternal life as if they understand what eternity means. Maybe you will have eternal life, but eternity is pain? So, you're now stuck with a life and must deal with eternity. These are thoughts you've no doubt had but cover with a sheet to never see them.

Yes, I've seen those thoughts you're having even now. Your thoughts waver towards wanting to know where Thomas Lewis is right now. You've thought about putting this book down completely because the author maybe comes off pretentious. The author doesn't have an extensive educational background to back up his claims and has no evidence to think the way he does. But neither does a layman reading the Bible for the first time. The layman expected to have years of theology to understand what it is God wants his people to know, an everyday person attempting to find answers. People spend lifetimes attempting to understand words from religious texts and yet we expect everyday people to buy into their ideology without question.

Thomas Lewis was a Christian. Which means, normally, he shouldn't think of such nonsensical questions. But seeing David walk behind the curtain has thrown him into a frenzy of wanting to know more. It's not that Tom isn't a part of a religion which doesn't allow for questions. On the contrary, Christianity often encourages people to question. But only questions that are preapproved by prior theologians who have sought answers. For example, it is perfectly okay and natural to question the existence of God. It is not okay, however, to question if one's own consciousness *is* God. It is normal to ask why bad things happen to good people. But it is not okay to ask if God is evil and, let us say, Satan is the righteous. These questions undoubtedly have answers. But to ask these questions is offensive in the eyes of the Church.

These comments aren't meant to sway the Christian faith. Christianity allows for some form of questioning which isn't always the case for every religion. I don't think the author has much experience outside of Christianity. So, most of the book will likely revolve around the Christian religion. But it is an overwhelming statistic Tom would end up being Christian anyway. Unless he was chosen to be a Christian by his God and raised with Christian values. And if Christianity is the *right* religion then that would be convenient. If it is the wrong religion and some other higher being other than the Christian God chose Tom to be Christian, then why? Was it to have him question his beliefs to one day fall into the right religion? Would that be an accurate judgement to make on a person if they were simply raised in the wrong religion? What makes an accurate judgement in the first place? But I digress. Tom is a Christian. It's something the author knows and so that's the story we follow. I can't blame Tom for that, nor can I blame him for being raised a Christian when it may or may not be the right religion.

Although, following this story, the author didn't realize Tom's closest friend would be an atheist. What an interesting stone cast into the pond of his thoughts. The author watches the story unfold much like the reader does. The author is just the first to read the story. He is the captain of a ship taking us into unexplored waters. He didn't create the waters; he only maneuvers the waves. Much like you, the author is surprised to find Tom brushing his teeth in a communal bathroom near his cot.

It wasn't a comfortable cot. When he first saw it, Eric told him this was the bottom where everyone started. You could work hard and make a name for yourself, eventually moving into your own nicer home.

But for now, this was where Tom was going to have to sleep. The cot didn't look uncomfortable at first sight. It was a small dark green bed in the middle of a large room housing some twenty people in the Community Center. A large window on one of the walls revealed their communal garden and few farm animals. These were sold in their own block for money to spend in Acedia.

Tom did feel his neighbors were a little too friendly on the first night. He was wedged between two exceptionally large men on either side of him. Both the men were very masculine. Tom would know, he was very acquainted with each man's large pecs as he felt suffocated the entire night. Tom's flabby body easily moved to accommodate their gigantic muscles, but he couldn't help to think he would sleep better without their pressure. On top of the pain, Tom could hear the faint sounds of sniffles and snores throughout the room. All of these factors made it impossible for Tom to find any sleep. So, he found himself in the restroom early in the morning.

Tom quickly found out he was not a morning person. But he felt if he were to get almost no sleep he might as well get first run at the communal restroom. Spitting in the sink, Tom stared at his brown eyes in the mirror. They were curious and almost black eyes. He'd heard once how eyes were the windows to the soul. But when Tom stared into his eyes, he saw a man he didn't recognize. A man who seemed more physical than himself. He no longer noticed when pieces of information suddenly came into his head. He was becoming accustom to a non-linear existence.

If Tom was an atheist, like his best friend Eric. He wouldn't believe in the drivel of souls. Unless the old saying meant eyes were incredibly discerning to find people's true intentions, in which case this were true. Tom's eyes did not look like windows to the soul. Within Tom's eyes as he closely watched them, he felt as though he were inside the room and someone else peered in. He looked around the bathroom behind him then back into the mirror. His eyes, with brown honey swirling around his black pupil, did not show a mysterious world of souls and spirituality. They looked alive. Tom's heart started to beat quicker as he felt the danger he saw in the mirror. It was the danger a child gets from looking at lions behind cages at the zoo. He was safe, but he knew something lived beyond the mirror staring back into his own eyes.

Tom shook his head and looked at the sink his hands rested on. They were incredibly clean. He was not a man of hard labor. He almost felt like a man who controlled a robot as he stared at his body. He became even more aware of his consciousness and felt as though it's all he was as he simply controlled the meat suit around him. Maybe his eyes weren't windows, maybe hands were windows. Or maybe there was no soul. Maybe whatever stared back at him was god testing him.

Knock knock. Someone was at the bathroom door. The people of the Community Center were slowly waking up, meaning it was time for Tom to start his day. Part of him wanted to immediately call Eric and ignore meeting his parents that day. Couldn't he get by with just the one friend? Why should he meet his parents? He already has someone to help him. His parents were fellow Christians though, maybe he could see their side of beliefs. In those few seconds, Tom realized he was also very grumpy in the mornings.

He didn't like Eric's belief of atheism. He didn't like the idea that something wasn't in control. But which belief could be right? Maybe they were all wrong. Maybe they were all right. Tom sighed in the middle of the bathroom. He walked to the door and opened it. To his surprise, it wasn't anyone he'd seen from his community. He didn't see the person who knocked at first. Looking down Tom was startled to find an incredibly old man fidgeting in place. This was odd in the Community Center but not unheard of. People who arrived at the Community Center arrived at the precise age they were supposed to. The old man wore tattered clothes and was almost exclusively skin and bone. He had a crazed look on his face with a large smile revealing two rows of teeth barely hanging onto the gums above and below. Taken back by the sight of the elderly man, Tom made an audible gasp of fright. The man suddenly grabbed Tom by the shoulder squeezing him tightly. Tom was very confused by the interaction and frantically looked for anyone else in the hall. There was no one. There was only this crazed old man and Tom. The man kept whispering to himself and also looked around. Tom had a feeling this was for some other reason than to look for other people.

"No piece... only one... no one knows... empty piece... only one... no piece... no one knows," the man frantically whispered as his old decrepit hands warily reached into his torn jacket. With a swift motion, the old man held into the air a single puzzle piece. He held it between his index finger and thumb now smiling even larger as if he held onto a piece of gold. Slowly, the man lowered the piece in front of Tom. Matching the energy of the old man, Tom slowly reached out his hand and took the piece. The moment Tom held it the old man jumped in the air only to dart away down the hallway. Tom watched him leap as if to hide from everyone who would soon wake up.

Tom opened his palm and looked at the small puzzle piece. It wasn't a corner piece but a center piece. It had three black lines curved to different sides filled with white space in between. There was nothing special about the piece that Tom could tell. He flipped it over and saw its cardboard backing. Nothing would have distinguished it from any other puzzle piece. Tom shrugged his shoulders and put it into his pocket.

Peering into the hallway, Tom walked down the opposite way of the old man. Tom didn't think the man seemed dangerous, but it was someone he didn't care to encounter again. He made his way down the corridor and saw people were just now lining up to use the different restrooms. He passed various people who were yawning and shuffling to the lines still in their pajamas. This gave Tom a small amount of superiority. He'd been awake for over an hour already. He was wide awake and ready to start the day.

Waltzing down the corridor he found his confidence again, forgetting about the old man. He pulled out his phone and saw that he had three missed calls and an unread text from someone. All of them were from his parents, the people that were supposed to usher him into the Community Center. They were the people who were supposed to show him the glory of food and the sugary taste of carbonated beverages he already tried with Eric the night before. Tom smiled, he didn't know these people, but could see from their calling and texts that they cared. The text beneath the small digital envelope on his phone was awaiting his eyes. He looked and saw it was from his dad. He opened it and read aloud.

"Were are you," Tom whispered as he walked down the hallway. You didn't catch a typo in the authors grammar either (although I'm sure plenty can be found). Tom's dad most certainly misspelled the word "where" forgetting the "h". There were two things that came to Tom's mind when he saw this typo, the first was that Tom's father was strict. It was a very straight forward message. This meant that Tom's father was serious. On the other hand, maybe his father just didn't know how to effectively use his phone. Something Tom could most certainly help him with.

As Tom walked he passed a large glass window reflecting off his phones screen causing Tom to look up. There was nothing on the other side of the glass, just a brick wall. It was a poorly constructed Community Center. But as he kept walking, he passed another window. On the other side of the glass twelve men and women were rolling out miniature rectangular mats on the ground. The women wore tight pants and tops, the men wore baggy basketball shorts. The woman at the front of the room stood in a "T" pose. She was the woman from the bus. Tom smiled and continued watching her. She was beautiful in every way he could think of. But as romantic as Tom was unable to be in this moment of ignorance, he only wanted to be with her.

She noticed him, staring, probably coming across as creepy from your standards. But Tom was new to the Community Center, only having spent a night there. He remembered just how attracted he was to her on the bus. She'd already been in the Community Center several months now. She looked at him and smiled. She turned her head away from him like she did on the bus hoping she wasn't caught staring. This reminded Tom of when she did the same thing on the bus. Tom stared at her, unknowing societies rules of staring. Quickly, he looked around the window for any sign of what they were doing but couldn't find anything. Whatever they were doing looked very peculiar and self-satisfying. He mentally noted where it was so he could return to see her again. But, for now, Tom had to meet his parents at their small section of paradise in the Community Center.

Tom continued walking down the hallway. He passed by more blocks where people sold various goods. As he kept walking he noticed the blocks were built a little nicer from where he started. Concrete turned into some places constructed from wood and into some blocks being built out of red brick. Some of the hallways were filled with bustling people and some were completely empty. He walked past another food court he hadn't seen before. He saw windows peering into a garden being tended by a few people. He walked by an old woman who caught his attention. The only other old person he'd seen so far. She knitted something on a rocking chair. But Tom kept walking.

Chapter VII

The Rabbit and the Bear

Something new caught Tom's attention more than anything else as he walked. He found an entrance to a large courtyard about the size of one of the food courts. On either side of the entrance were giant pillars helping up a stone slab. Etched into the slab was something written in another language Tom didn't recognize. The areas construction looked much different than the rest of Acedia he'd seen so far. It looked like ancient stones constructing the area. But Tom noticed the courtyard was almost made to look as if it were old. The stone was actually just normal concrete found in his own section of Acedia.

Curious, Tom peered inside. He heard lots of screaming and yelling. Not terrifying screaming as if anyone were in any danger. This was angry conflicted screaming. In front of a large building beyond the entrance, he saw a group of men and women in suits holding up fists and screaming at each other. They surrounded something looking downward as if they were witnessing a dog fight. Tom knew he shouldn't divert too far from the path to see his parents, but he wanted to know what the commotion was about. He slowly pushed himself past a few people to see what was in the middle of the large gathering. What he found; he did not expect.

In the middle of the group was a portrait of a large bear. It was not a real bear mind you but was a portrait of a sleeping bear next to a large cave. The bear's painted eyes were shut as it slept peacefully. Something else was in the middle of the group as well. Tom saw another portrait of yet another animal sitting next to the bears portrait. It was a small furry creature painted hopping into the air much more energetic than the bear. It was a rabbit. In the rabbits hand was a large stick looking as though it would swing down with its hop. This was very comical to Tom and he started to smile. He didn't see why everyone was so upset. The portrayal of each painting was meant to go with one another. The bunny acted as a sort of alarm for the bear who peacefully slept. The bear was clearly enjoying its nap but would soon be woken by the rabbit who was about to hit him over the head with a stick. Tom looked around at the men and women screaming. They weren't fighting over what exactly the bear and rabbit were doing, they were fighting over taking the bear and replacing it with another animal. One side fought for the rabbit and the other side fought for the bear.

Tom was having a very confusing morning. First, it was the puzzle piece he was given, and now people were fighting over paintings of a bear and a rabbit. He touched someone on the shoulder. They quickly turned to look at him with a fiery anger in their eyes.

"Do you know what's going on?" Tom asked innocently. The woman did not answer his question but asked something else, confusing Tom further.

"What? You're with the rabbit? It's fake! It's all fake! Just look at it! If you don't like the bear painting, then just leave!" the woman screamed in Tom's face. Tom barely made out what the woman yelled over the roar of the thunderous crowd. Maybe the woman was one in a million. Tom made his way to the other side of the crowd and tapped on another person's shoulder. Quickly, the man turned around with the same fire in his eyes.

"What is going on here?" Tom asked diligently trying to get to the bottom of the situation.

"Oh, that's typical! Straight white male, too high and mighty to know what this is about. Fascist pig! Racist! The rabbit wouldn't poke the bear if it wasn't, you know, a BEAR! We need to get rid of that bear and put in a rabbit like before!" the man yelled ignoring Tom's question. Tom made his way back out from the crowd and at the entrance again. He put his hand on the stone and sighed at the sight of everyone. Most people outside the entrance looked to mostly ignore what was happening inside. They went about their business and genuinely tried to be kind to one another. Tom walked back out into the hallway and reached into his pocket. He held onto the puzzle piece. He felt an odd sense of comfort from the high-tension situation he was just in.

Finding his path again, he kept strolling until he found himself at a mid-tier residential block of the Community Center. It wasn't gated, but the normal concrete floor suddenly turned into a red brick stretching far into the housings. Doors on either side of the hallway lined to its end. This was a place of relatively wealthy people who could afford small homes separated from one another. This was where Tom's parents lived. Inside one of these nice apartment-like courters lived the people who would answer many of Tom's questions. He almost completely forgot about beliefs. He wanted to see what his parents would be like.

Tom walked past door after door seeing each apartment had enough room in the front for a small garden and a welcome mat. It was calming to see the neighborly atmosphere after the passionate anger he just encountered. Along the walk Tom slowly realized he couldn't remember exactly what apartment number his parents were. He thought the memory would come to him but for whatever reason it didn't. In the distance, he saw a short man a little older than himself standing outside a red door waving at Tom. The man held a water hose running inside their courters and slowly gave water to the beautiful flowers outside. A great smile split across this man's face and his right hand motioned back and forth at the sight of Tom. This was undoubtedly Tom's father. Tom slowly walked up to him with a glow across his face staring at his dad. He looked at the apartment and recognized it immediately. This was home for Tom. This was a part of Tom's childhood.

Tom's father was a good and healthy age. He had a little pepper in his thick mustache but wasn't elderly. There was age in his eyes attached with joyous wisdom. He clearly had seen a few things in his existence and could share with Tom the ends and outs of life. Tom smiled back at his dad.

"Tommy my boy! It's so great to have you! Come on in your mothers making her famous poppyseed muffins," Tom's dad yelled at him as he walked into the apartment. "Oh, that's food. She's so excited for your first taste to be her poppyseed muffins," he turned around and told Tom as he followed his dad.

The red door reminded Tom of growing up. He remembered when his mom couldn't decide between green, blue, or red. One day she came home, and his father had painted it red without her knowing. It was good to see it again. The small apartment looked similar to most apartments. But this was his parents place, and the place he grew up.

"Let me look at you. Boy, I don't know who gave you that growth gene, but it clearly wasn't me," Tom's dad chuckled. He smiled at the joke. Tom was glad to find out his dad had a sense of humor. It wasn't like the normal sense of humor he joked with Eric about. It was a tame fatherly sense of humor.

"Look at me! Look at you! I didn't get your height, but I got your chiseled jaw line!" Tom broke the silence and continued the tame joke with his dad. The two men did not share a chiseled jaw line. In fact, both of the men's faces were nicely rounded.

Tom's dad embraced him with a hug. This, confused Tom slightly but the warmth of his father's hug calmed down any of his thoughts. It didn't matter to Tom that the hug made no logical sense. What mattered was how he felt when his dad put his arms around him. It was a different feeling. It was as if the memories of the apartment were wrapping their arms around him telling him it would be okay.

"Tommy!" a shriek of a high-pitched woman came from the other room. Tom's father let go of him and the awkwardness returned.

"Hear that Tommy? That's my beautiful wife. Your beautiful mother," Tom's father told him as they stood in the entry way of the apartment. A shadow of a figure came through the tiled kitchen only a few feet away. There she was... Tom's mother. She was the epitome of motherhood. She was a large, rounded woman with an apron wrapped around her waist caked in flower. She wore no makeup and her hair tied loosely in a bun on her head. Tom was immediately struck with joy. Not the sense of joy he felt with his father, but an overall warmth of welcoming overcame Tom as he stared at her. She put her hands on her chest and her bottom lip shook as tears filled her eyes.

"My boy!" she exclaimed as she came closer to him giving Tom a big hug. Hers was much tighter than his fathers. But it was just as accepted. Tom stepped away from them both and grinned. All of Tom's worries seemed to melt away in their presence. He forgot about Eric, he forgot about the puzzle piece, and he forgot about the terrifying people arguing. Most importantly, Tom forgot about the ominous curtain that would one day consume them all.

Chapter VIII

Freely Chosen or Chosen Freely

"Heavenly father, I do not understand this reality you have created. I've spent existence following you and everything you stand for and yet there I was, faced with the devil himself, and could do nothing to it. And even still, at least *he* showed himself to me...," Clive began his prayer in a hopeful wish but paused the moment he was starting to accuse the God he believed. Clive is a good man with a good heart who, in many ways, is much like our protagonist Tom. They both seek answers and want to understand existence more than they currently do. Although, Clive does have more of a foundational answer to step off. Whereas Tom is beginning to lean to more practical and analytical understanding of existence. Both are valid and most fall into Clive's category.

For a moment Clive paused at his prayer and remembered a diagram he was shown when he was younger. It was a diagram a teacher showed him about how the world actually works. He smirked. Clive remembered how the conversation started with his distaste for psychology. But he never really understood why he didn't care for psychology. Most of his colleagues in college and even his parents told him he should work towards being a psychologist. But he was always frustrated with psychology classes.

"It's based on assumption," the teacher told him. Clive asked what the professor meant. So, he drew four circles connected to each other by a single line. The first circle the professor wrote the word "philosophy". He turned from the white board to face Clive who sat in the empty classroom.

"Philosophy is the start. It's the question of everything. What is existence? Why do we exist? What is consciousness? Why do we question?" the short professor told Clive. He then turned back to the whiteboard and wrote in the second circle the words "moral Philosophy". He then changed the line connecting the two circles and made it an arrow. Showing the progression from "philosophy" to "moral philosophy".

"Once we have answers for philosophy, we can use it as a foundation for moral philosophy. What is right and what is wrong? What makes them right and what makes them wrong? Is your right the same as my right? And we only *know* these questions to be true because of what we learn in the first circle... philosophy," the professor explained with these questions only as examples. This time the professor quickly scribbled the word "theology" into the third circle. Clive's ears pricked at the word. It related to something he loved to study. The professor, again, drew an arrow showing the progression between moral philosophy and theology.

"And when we have answers for moral philosophy, we inevitably ask where they came from. Who created morals? Who created any of it? Is there something pulling the strings in our minds? Does this 'being' dictate moral philosophy?" the professor paused and pointed to Clive. "And what of the ballot in your pocket right now? The one in my own pocket. You know just as well as I do we wrote the ballot. It wasn't written by anyone but us. So, what makes any belief on the ballot different if I said I created existence?" the professor paused at his example, knowing full well the belief that "you are God" was already on the ballot to be voted on. But this didn't answer Clive's question about why he had such a terrible issue with the subject of psychology. So, the professor turned around again and wrote inside the last circle the word "psychology". Drawing one last arrow he connected all four circles. The professor set his marker down.

"Psychology makes claims about the way we interact with those around us and the way our minds operate. It makes claims about consciousness but based on assumptions made in the previous circles. The foundation has yet to have any real answers. The truth is, we don't know anything. We don't know what consciousness is or why we question. We don't know what existence is or why we exist. Any answer someone gives you will be an assumption they made about existence by following a string of logic they deemed to fit a narrative they understand best. This circle...," the professor said pointing to "philosophy". "...has yet to be answered. And until we have truth, then it's all assumption," the professor finished. Clive could see the mental toll the subject took on his professor. The professor was a shorter and older man. Someone who was around the corner from retiring at the time of speaking to him. And soon, Clive knew the elderly man would walk towards the curtain to the center of the Community Center just as everyone else. But what he said did make sense to Clive. He could never grasp why people thought they understood anything about existence when nothing foundational was ever true.

As Clive prayed to the God he desperately believed in, he reached into his pocket and clasped onto a small puzzle piece. A small token to remember where his foundations were. Yes, it was similar to the puzzle piece Tom had in his own pocket. Two different shapes, two different patterns on the pieces, but presumably the same puzzle. A foundation for Clive to clasp onto so he could always *know* something instead of just *believing* in something. Something physical reminding him of his own faith perhaps. Something you, the reader, will learn more about in coming chapters and how you also hold onto a puzzle piece tucked in your own pocket.

"...And maybe this is why you do not reveal yourself to me. Maybe it all hinges on faith for me to follow blindly in your stead so I may feel your presence if not but once in my existence. So be it. So be your will if evil to exist and so be your will if I have nothing but faith to clutch onto instead of answers to any questions. You say to seek, and I will find. Find what? Haven't I found you? Haven't I sought and found the evil plaguing the Community Center only to be unprepared by your own doing?" Clive said pausing once again. Realizing his words were becoming passive aggressive towards a great God he believed to be the creator of existence.

I'm certainly not one to disagree with him. If I were to pray to a God I believed in like Clive did, then I too would be worried about making any accusations towards it. But funny enough, Clive pauses over accusing a God he only believes exists, but he does not let go of a puzzle piece that solidifies his belief either. An internal struggle clearly reads across Clive's face. Anger boils in the man as he wants to scream at the God who gave him existence.

"And which God is it!" Clive takes his hand out of his pocket squeezing his puzzle piece tighter and tighter. Veins bulge on his wrist as his fists shake pushing against his forehead. Hidden behind is a mind struggling greatly to understand which belief is correct and which God he prays to.

"Which God is true...," he whispers into the silence only to be met with more silence. Clive is not alone though. As much as he would like to think he is. Tom questions many things as Clive does. If we want to really get into a fourth wall break, Clive isn't alone because you are reading about him also. Of course, you can't respond really. But I'm here with him.

Well, I supposed you could respond to him if you wrote your own book with the same character Clive and wanted to see where the story led. And if you did write your own story who would say which one was any truer than the other? If you wrote a story where Clive got his answer from God then would it be truer? And in that story, would it be the true God of the real world or a fictional one made up for a story? This new god added to the multitudes of beliefs written on the ballot for people to choose from. But I supposed it isn't your book. I'll be there in yours if you decide to write it. I'll be interested to meet the god of that book.

"I will never know the truth behind you," Clive said as he opened his hand revealing the small puzzle piece. His eyes didn't take notice to the room he kneeled in. It was a small one bedroom apartment he lived in. Clive wasn't one who could afford an entire house like Tom's parents. But still made enough of himself to afford a small place. But he did not see his room right now. He only stared at the puzzle piece.

"No one will ever know the truth. Going behind the curtain may be the only way to ever know," he whispered to himself.

Which is untrue. But I see the steps he took to find himself in that conclusion. I can't really blame him, and neither should you. The man was just dealt an incredible hit to his ego on the third floor. I know it didn't seem like much considering you were just introduced to Clive's story. But he was searching for most his existence for the third floor. He watched his professor drive himself mad over the very questions Clive struggled with now and to come back empty handed was only proof Clive might end up mad just like his old professor.

But the problem with Clive's theory about understanding what's after the curtain is the same problem he faced in the moment of his current existence. Because if he doesn't know where he is now, how could he ever trust where he is after the curtain no matter how satisfying it may be? Afterall, he could go past the curtain and see exactly what he believes true. Everything he marked on the ballot came up correct and his politician won the election. Great. But how does he know what that existence is? How does he know he isn't having the curtain pulled over his eyes to something else really happening? Even after going beyond the curtain, wouldn't he also be wanting to know more and never have the conclusion to these questions?

Oh, never mind, he's actually headed towards the curtain right now. That's probably not a good sign. I mean, I like talking about philosophical ideas, but it looks to me like Clive is definitely headed towards the center of the Community Center. It won't take long for Clive to reach the middle of the Community Center. Although he does live in Phestiles, a division of the Community Center no one has spoken much about.

Phestiles has the same basic structure as Acedia, with various blocks where people live. But Phestiles was ruled by a king and its citizens are not as passive as Acedia. The king was ever proud of his ruling. Posters of himself plastered across every wall for the people to continually know who owned them. The hallways and corridors of Phestiles were covered with a red tint. It's as if you were constantly wearing glasses with red lenses. This unnatural sight in Phestiles was caused by the collective anger its citizens had. As Clive walked, it was all normal to him. He saw people arguing in the streets over petty things. He saw people hitting each other until one would fall to the ground trying to get up. People crouched in corners as Clive walked by trying to ignore their needs. They paid no attention to him as most of us wouldn't. Clive still clutched onto his old puzzle piece as he passed by the various people. He didn't look like a crazed old man but a man with a vision and a destination. I don't think the destination at the center of the Community Center will end exactly where he thinks it will lead him. At least, it's not going to lead him where it wants him to lead him. I don't want it to lead to him behind the curtain. So, it's not going to.

How odd is that though. Here we have Clive with full intentions on going behind the curtain to end his existence because he's reached the end of his rope. He clutches onto the only thing he knows to be real, a puzzle piece in his hand. And yet, I don't want him to. Does this mean Clive doesn't have free will? Because I can guarantee he's not going behind that curtain even though he wants to. He's not going to end his existence. Let's see what happens. Maybe we'll finally have at least one answer to whether or not Clive has free will or not.

Clive rushes past certain people. Phestiles shops are opened with short lines and people begging for food. He sees people preaching on wooden boxes occasionally in a way to spread the word of their belief. He sees those same people pushed from their boxes in the name of religious superiority. This only makes it worse for Clive. His eyes begin to frantically find the next hallways leading to the center of the Community Center. He holds the puzzle piece close to his chest and is starting to look like a drug addict as he finally stumbles into one of the corridors leading into the park.

He stops. This is it. This is where he would make his final goodbyes to nothing. His family wouldn't know he left until they did. And his friends would probably meet him on the other side or at the beginning of his existence someday. He touched the wall with his left hand while holding the puzzle piece in his right. Sliding his hand against the rough dark concrete he felt the graffiti as he walked. The red tint of Phestiles slowly faded as candles lit his way into the bright opening where the curtain hung. As he walked Clive saw pictures lining the ceiling. Pictures of people who'd past naturally through the corridor and into perceived oblivion. All with different beliefs and different votes on their ballots. But there was only one way for Clive to ever know for certain. So, there was only one way Clive could see from here.

How do I stop him from doing it? And if I stop him from going through the curtain does it mean he doesn't have free will or did I only redirect his attention to something else? Causing him to change his mind about the subject. Because there is a way I'm going to stop him from going through the curtain. It mostly has to do with changing when events take place in the book. But that would be like saying if you stopped a person from killing themselves in your reality, then that person doesn't have free will because they didn't go through with their original plan. And just because I know Clive is going to do it without any interference from myself, doesn't mean he doesn't have free will. Basically, just because I know what's going to happen doesn't stop Clive from having free will. Knowledge of events doesn't change whether or not someone has the choice to make them or not.

Clive steps onto the grass fully ready to walk through the curtain. He relaxes himself for a moment and straightens himself out. He feels as though he is ready. Holding onto his jacket with the puzzle piece tightly in his palm he begins walking towards the center of the park. The curtain hangs peacefully. Just as before, various people are walking into it never to be seen again. Cries, laughter, and chatter can be heard throughout the circular park. Clive walks down the hill and hears the grass crunch with each step. His intention is clear. His free will is made known.

But... he notices someone. He notices a person sitting by themselves just staring blankly at the curtain. No tears, no laughs, no friends, just by themselves in a trance. This person sits on a hill not too far from where Clive walks. Someone who reminded him much of himself as he used to do the very same. He used to sit for hours staring at the black curtain in the distance, never getting too close.

Does Clive have the choice to keep walking and ignore the man? Yes, he does. But he doesn't and he's made that choice on his own as well. He stops a few feet behind the young man who looks thoroughly interested in the curtain. He wonders how he should say hello. The young man's eyes stared directly into the curtain. He was clearly questioning everything Clive had before. The man was simply lost. And, before Clive was to go beyond the curtain. Maybe stopping and having a chat wouldn't be such a terrible thing. Clive put the puzzle piece back into his pocket and sat down next to the man.

Chapter IX

A Much Needed Guide

Tom bit into the fluffy poppyseed muffin his mother baked for him hours prior. She had handed it to him across the dark wooden table sitting in the small kitchen of their home. The kitchen was decorated with various shades of yellow. A theme of squares and circles popped in black contrast against the singular color of a light yellow. This gave the impression of a bumblebee, her favorite insect. Tom didn't have a favorite insect and thought it was odd for his mom to have one. But she always told him bees were what kept food on their table.

Tom had never been inside a kitchen before. He knew of their existence because his own communal living space had one. But only the cooks were allowed inside. Something he immediately noticed was scent.

He realized it had always been with him since he began existing, but the sudden aroma of his mother's baking struck him as especially delightful. Tom did remember a smell which stuck out to him before. But it was not pleasant like the one he currently enjoyed. It was the smoke from Eric's cigarette outside the Community Center. I don't want to go over it again. We're in the kitchen now. The smell of the poppyseed muffin he held would be latched to the memory of his mother and in retrospect, the very concept of belonging.

Staring at the poppyseed muffin in the palm of his hand Tom knew he hadn't the heart to tell his mother it wasn't the first time he tasted food. Sitting across from him, she quietly held her breath waiting for his reaction. His eyes lit up to the lemony fluffy taste swirling in his mouth. Tom's eyes closed as he felt the rush of sweet beauty. This muffin was delicious. But more than that, it was distinct from the chicken he tasted the night before. He could feel something with this muffin. He opened his eyes and looked at his mother sitting across from him. The palm of her hand was on her chest as she smiled at the sight of her son enjoying her food. Tom looked down at the muffin and made a small connection. He felt as though he could literally taste the belonging his mother gave him. He could taste the love she had for her son in the cooking. It was beautiful. He lived in this moment without any questions berating his mind.

"I knew it. I knew you'd love my cooking," she said standing up from the table waving her index finger. She walked over to the fridge and poured a glass of liquid. From Tom's perspective it was some sort of white liquid. While wondering what it was, his throat constricted. Tom instantly felt a new sensation. His mouth dried as if he'd eaten sand. His lips cracked and begged for something, but he didn't know what. It felt as though he needed air but the more he breathed, the worse it became. He needed something to quench whatever this sensation was. His mother walked over to him and handed him the glass of cold liquid. Tom quickly took it and put his mouth against the glass. Tom realized very quickly he didn't want to ever feel the sensation of "thirst" ever again. Sure, he had a drink the night before. But Tom wasn't thirsty. Thirst was something new to him.

"You know, I always believed food would unite the Community Center. It would only take a good meal, and Phestiles and Acedia would stop the ridiculous fighting," she said sitting back down on the other side of the table.

"Unite the Community Center?" Tom asked, biting into the muffin again. This time, he kept his glass of milk close by to hopefully ensure he wouldn't deal with thirst again.

"Oh goodness, it seems like every day there's something new to be mad about. Phestiles is growing and Acedia fights for whoever they think has the best painting. Nobody ever gets along," she said leaning her chin on the palm of her hand. She looked concerned with how the Community Center was doing.

"Is it all about the ballot? The different beliefs?" Tom asked hoping to understand how the people of existence lived. She sighed at this.

"Some of it is. Phestiles is a scary place where people go when they don't understand their own beliefs. It usually makes them cruel or helpless. Lord knows I've lived there before," she said.

"You've lived in Phestiles?" Tom asked his mother. She was very open about her past and future.

"Oh yes. Your father and I lived there for a very long time. Constantly fighting over every little thing," she told her son.

"What brought you to Acedia? Why come to Acedia?" he asked her politely.

"Well, your father and I decided one day we didn't want to live like that anymore. We would choose to believe our God regardless of understanding. People think if we all believe the same thing then it will unify us," she said as she picked at one of the muffins sitting on the plate in front of her. She seemed to be distracted and bored with the conversation. Tom could see the conversation was old for her. She may have had it before or would have it soon to come. It seemed every belief had just as much chance as every other at knowing what was behind the curtain. Putting so much stock into finding out which one was right would force yourself into Phestiles. But Tom never considered what would happen if everyone did believe the same.

"Would it? I mean, would having a centralized belief unify Acedia and Phestiles?" he asked her. He began chewing the final bite of the poppyseed muffin. She thought about his question for a moment and about how she would answer. It's not something she gave a lot of thought to in the past. The dilemma in her head was her ability to say no without diminishing her own belief in the process.

"I don't think so. I don't think God intends for us all to be the same people," she answered not knowing if it were the right answer. But she did believe it.

"Why would it matter? We still wouldn't be any closer to *knowing* instead of *believing*," Tom said leaning back in his chair. He wasn't thinking too heavily into the conversation. He acted like a child following breadcrumbs of each question she tried to answer.

"No, you're right. We wouldn't know. But belief and knowing are not exclusive from one another. You must *believe* before you can *know*," she told him. He could sense conviction in her voice.

"You're saying the truth is whatever you believe?" he asked her. She shook her head slowly with a warm smile.

"I didn't say that at all. I'm saying belief comes before knowing. I believe in Jesus Christ which will turn into knowing," she said to Tom. He didn't want to go down the rabbit hole of whether her religion was right or not. They both knew there was no way to prove undoubtedly any religion was right. He was more interested in the innerworkings of existence itself.

"So, you don't think everyone should believe your belief is the right one? Not everyone should believe in

Jesus Christ?" he asked her. She was taken back by his almost accusatory tone of voice. But she had known Tom a very long time and knew how his conversations always went.

"It isn't that Christianity is right or wrong. There is no belief that is right or wrong because there is an absolute truth that circumvents the ballot," she said. Now this was something that took Tom into a whirlwind of thoughts. He subconsciously wondered where his curiosity came from and he now understood it came from his mother. A silence fell between the two of them as he digested what she said.

He looked around the kitchen. Its yellow patterns warmed his heart. The physical space he took in the chair was becoming more noticeable to him. He looked at his mother who now looked at him with defensive eyes. He didn't feel like he was truly in the room. He felt like something piloting a body like he did when he stared in the mirror. Tom looked down at his hands and saw how far away from his consciousness they were. If he moved his right hand, then his right hand would move. If he moved his left hand, his left hand would move. He was a pilot. He looked around the kitchen again and saw the different designs of existence and wondered about what existence really was.

"But I can't even prove if any of this is existence," he said under his breath, staring at the matter around him. He leaned forward and touched the table. The feeling in his finger wasn't felt in his consciousness. It was only felt in his finger. This was a path that scared

Tom. This was a path he knew could lead to being an elderly man staring at a giant painting with no peace of mind. You'll understand that reference when Tom experiences it later.

"How do you mean?" his mother asked. She knew where the conversation would go mostly because she'd been in this conversation hundreds of times with Tom.

"This could be fake. It could be a simulation and none of it is real. Or maybe we're in an experiment. Maybe it's an experiment set up by far off aliens watching our every move. It could be that you're all robots and I have amnesia. Sure, I've learned about what humans are and the bodily anatomy. But would I ever know without stabbing someone and opening them up? I don't know what was before the bus and I don't know what's beyond the curtain. So, what rules out anything here? Hell, I could be dreaming all of this. Maybe I'm God and I wiped my memory to come live in the Community Center," Tom told her frantically, his eyes popping up from staring at his finger on the table. He remembered Eric saying something very similar when they first sat down together. But now these thoughts were becoming reality for Tom. She sighed, not out of annoyance, but because she too had these thoughts.

"You're not wrong. Anything could be anything else. It could be this isn't existence at all," she confirmed his hypothesis. This didn't take him off guard because he was too busy following the train of thoughts running in his mind. He remembered back to his conversation with Eric. How it ended with Eric and Tom disagreeing over the concept of "nothing". But Tom was taking it further.

"And you mom. How do I know you're real?" he asked taking his hand from the table and pointing at her. She smiled slightly at the blatant accusation.

"You don't Tom. There's no way for you to prove that I am real," she said. Tom didn't care to hear this though. He was hoping for her to have an answer. Some sort of proof that would put his mind at ease.

"The only thing I can prove is that I'm conscious....," he said slowly putting his head into his hands at the conclusion of his thoughts.

"Can you?" his mother said leaning forward. "If you're conscious then in what space are you conscious? If you can't even prove this space around you exists, then how do you know you're not another piece of the game? How do you know everything that makes you, yourself, isn't all a lie also? If I can't prove my consciousness to you and you can't prove yours to me, then you could be just as unreal as I am," she asked him. Tom's eyes widened. He thought he reached the end of his questions but instead his own mother showed him there was much more to this. He wanted his mom to be the normal mother who would comfort him. Instead, she pushed him further.

"I can't... I can't do it," Tom said sighing.

"So, tell me Tom. If you can't prove any of this is real, you can't prove I am real, and you can't even prove your own existence. What can you prove? What can you *know* instead of only *believe*?" she asked.

Tom thought about this for a minute. He couldn't prove anything. Existence was either a void or it wasn't. Existence was a lie, or it was something else. Tom's consciousness was a program, or it was real and free. His mother either loved him, or she was a part of a game set up to see how consciousness reacts to the curtain.

As the reader, you're going to need to think about this too. Tom is questioning everything he's ever been told. Humans live their lives off an unspoken trust for fellow humans to tell them about existence. And yet they can't even prove each other's consciousness. But what do Tom and his mother mean by consciousness? Surely you can speak to one another and know someone is conscious. But the question asked is how do you know someone experiences thought and feeling in the same way you do? You might say it's for the betterment of humanity for everyone to work together and live off these predetermined notions. But how does anyone know that life didn't exist before their birth and that it won't continue long after their death? And isn't it just as possible that you are the only one that exists? Sounds like a pretty selfish way to live, but only if it isn't true.

Some might say it's a juvenile viewpoint of the world. It begs the question why do anything at all or why care at all if everything is a fake world set up for one consciousness? But that's simple, it would be to live as comfortable as you can within the narrative of this world. But again, it isn't to prove all of this is fake but rather to show that every belief is just as valid as the last. So, what is provable? What can one *know* instead of *believe*? Tom could only come to one conclusion.

"Something... something is," Tom whispered under his breath. Those two simple words were the only thing Tom knew to be true with no belief needed. Whether "something" is what we perceive as existence or if it turns out to be fake. The only thing Tom knew without *belief* was that "something is". Whether that's true or not is debatable. But that's just what Tom thought. If I could make the shrug emoji in this book right now I would. But the author doesn't want to be the author known for putting an emoji in his book. I'll respect that.

"You asked me about Christianity being right or wrong. It's neither. It's nothing. But God? God is. He described himself as 'I am'. Not because he was so grand and powerful he was too indescribable. He said it because he is the 'something is' you said. He is and there is nothing else. Christianity isn't right or wrong. Only God is and he is always good," she told Tom. He looked up to his mother. This was a warm and welcoming answer to his questions. He hadn't the heart to tell her it didn't satisfy his philosophical thirst. Only because giving an answer to his dilemma of "something is" put doubt in the thing itself by simply being.

It's not something anyone can particularly grasp with ease. Tom feels the answer he was given doesn't satisfy the question because the "something is" or the "I am" God claims to be is doubtful. Only because it means the being of God is simply a being like the rest of us (regardless of however powerful he may be). But what Tom failed to see was his mother attempted to explain that God was not a being. He is being. Then the next question would be "What is being?". Tom instead chose to be comfortable in the question he already had.

"The idea everyone should have one central belief is a very time centric belief in itself," his mother said breaking the silence. Being disappointed in what she told him earlier he latched onto something he hadn't heard before. A word she said. It was strong and mysterious and bounded around his mind looking for a place to land.

"Time?" he asked her curiously. She looked up from picking at the muffin in front of her.

"Oh, I'm sorry Tom. I've never been a mother before, so I forget you're new," she said standing up. Tom thought about the term "time" she used. She returned shortly and placed a map on the table.

She sat back down and leaned across to show Tom. It was the map of a large building. It wasn't any certain shape with a specific label. It had several different sides making up its walls. They all pointed in different directions and connected just as randomly. Some of the walls jutted out from the sides as if it were from poor construction. Surrounding the building was a large chasm circling it's jutted walls. On the outside of the chasm was a large area labeled as the forest with no indicator as to what it was. Inside the building Tom saw many rooms. Large rooms, small rooms, rooms with beds and rooms that looked important. He saw the divisions of each block where people could live and enjoy their small communes. He knew deep down what he looked at was the Community Center.

"This is where you came in. Gate number 2...," she said pointing to the edge of the Community Center. Her index finger rested on one of the bridges that came across the chasm. There were six bridges in total with only three entrances and three exits. A bridge would stretch across the chasm then curve around back over the chasm and into the forest. "...I still remember the first time you came across," she said as tears formed in her eyes. "Anyway, here is where you start out and here is where we are now," her finger moved across the page to where Tom's cot was. She then swiftly moved her finger to where his parents lived. It was the first time Tom had seen the Community Center in its entirety. It was huge. He tried to remember the hallways he took that morning.

"What is that room?" he asked pointing at the place he'd seen the people fighting over paintings. She followed his finger to where he pointed.

"Oh, that's one of the many political rooms. Where people go to discuss how the Community Center should be ran. It's another reason why people are constantly fighting. Thankfully Acedia has reduced it to only a few courtyards," she explained. "Now, 'Time' is on the second floor of the Community Center. There's only one way up and it's this elevator," she told him. Tom was very confused though.

"But what is it?" he asked her. She thought about how to answer his question. From the point of view of someone who'd never witnessed "time", it was very difficult to explain.

"Don't you wonder why we weren't there to welcome you to existence? Or why you have memories of me, but you've only been here a day? Maybe you have future memories already but haven't seen them yet," she asked him. He didn't think about it much. He accepted how existence worked and how he sometimes just knew things before they happened. It's how he met Eric or met Eric again. It's how he knew Clive right now but hasn't met him yet. But the strangest thing yet, that forced him into all these questions of existence, was seeing the strange man walk through the curtain immediately.

"Yeah, it's been kind of strange. I saw a man called David get right off the bus and walk straight to the curtain," Tom told her focusing on the map. His mother gasped as she leaned forward.

"You saw a suicide on your first few moments here? I'm so sorry Tommy. That's awful," she tried to comfort him. He felt her warmth. He did feel terrible for David but wanted more to understand the reasons behind David's actions. He wanted to know what propelled David into such a decision. Was it curiosity of knowing like Tom obsessed over? But David had only just started his existence. Why would he throw it away so soon?

"Someone was screaming his name. They were trying to get to him before it was too late... I didn't know what to do. They blamed me. They said I wasn't there for him," Tom quieted his voice in shock and respect for the passing of David. Tom's mother sighed at the example Tom gave to explain "Time".

"That person knew David before he existed. Just as you know Eric and you know us. Sometimes we go our entire existence knowing someone without meeting them. And sometimes we meet someone we will never really know," she responded quietly.

"What does that mean?" he asked her. He thought this was all knowledge you only received when you first started to exist. But if someone doesn't exist, then they can't know that person yet.

"There is a second floor to the Community Center called Time," she said. She could see Tom still didn't understand. "You can find David there. You can find his whole existence and possibly why he did what he did," she explained. Tom's eyes widened. All he needed to hear was that David was on the second floor. The curtain led to the second floor of the Community Center. Maybe it was some supernatural portal or technological transporter that sent you there. Could it really be that simple? He could waltz to the second floor, say hi to David, understand the Community Center, and be back to experience existence.

"How do I get there? I want to understand this," he asked, now with purpose behind his questions. She didn't want to show him the path to get there. He could see something held her back and didn't understand why.

"Tom, I don't know if it's such a good idea for you to go. Time is confusing. It's relative and you can get lost easily," she told him worriedly. Just as she said this, Tom's father entered the kitchen out of breath and sweaty. He wore basketball shorts and a blue t-shirt. He quickly opened the fridge door and took a red drink out.

"Where's Tom going?" his father asked taking a large gulp of the red liquid. He continued to take deep breaths. Tom didn't wonder what his father was doing because he knew his father was running on the treadmill in the spare bedroom. He saw him working out when leaving their house to see the second floor.

"Tom wants to go to the second floor," his mother said leaning back in her chair and crossing her arms. She looked directly at Tom, not disappointingly but worried.

"Time? He's been existing for what? A day and a half? I'd say it's about *time*. No pun intended," his father cracked a smile as he put the red drink down on the counter. His mother did not share in his father's delightful amusement.

"Coming from someone who was obsessed with Time," she spat at Tom's father. She very clearly had a problem with his father going to the second floor at one time. Whatever happened to his father was a great concern to his mother.

"Obsessed?" Tom asked. His father was now a little more rested and hydrated. He walked over to the table and took a seat next to Tom.

"Yes, I was obsessed with Time," he said. He looked at his wife who now could see her husband was taking this a little more seriously. "Time... is tricky. You can get so caught up with knowing exactly what everyone has done you forget about who everyone is. It doesn't work like that down here on the first floor. Up there, everything is linear. When you take away from the absolutely breathtaking worlds up there, you begin to see you're really just looking at a person's actions and see how or why someone else reacted," he attempted to explain.

Tom was looking more confused though. His father said the word "worlds" as if the second floor was entire planets. Tom's imagination couldn't stop thinking about the second floor of the Community Center now. If it was truly an experience unlike any other as his father explained it to be. His father could see the confusion and tried to think of another analogy.

"Here, it's like numbers...," his father took out a pen from a nearby drawer and wrote the numbers one, two, and three on the map. "If you count out loud one... two... three down here, then they are just individual numbers that exist...," he said as his pen moved to each number. "...But on the second floor in Time, there always must be a cause and effect. So, the number two can only happen because of one. Three can only happen because of two...," he continued as he pointed at the different numbers again. "...But again, down here, those three numbers are exactly what they are and where they are. Three is still three without one. The number two is still the number two without the number three...," his father explained. He looked at his wife who was also confused by the analogy for Time. Tom's father sighed. "...Honestly, it's something you have to experience for yourself. I think you should go," he told Tom. This didn't make his mother any happier as she hoped he would explain why it would be a bad idea.

Tom looked at the map of the Community Center. He was shown many confusing things and it seemed he might be able to find answers on the second floor. At least there he would be able to see David and understand the curtain a little more. He may come back down with questions still but at least he would have closed the door on a couple. His mother watched him and could tell there was no getting around her son wanting to go there. It wasn't that Time was going to harm him in any way. She only didn't want to see him become obsessed as his father did.

Tom stood up from his chair and kissed his mother on the forehead. "Thank you. I'll be back. I'll be safe," he told them. They both smiled at him.

"Don't you need to take the map?" she asked him.

"No need. I'm meeting someone soon who will help me get there," he replied almost surprising himself. He was starting to understand how things didn't operate linear on the first floor. He already had knowledge of someone he had yet to meet but knew he would.

"Remember this. Don't be concerned with Time itself. It does nothing. The only thing you can do is learn from the experiences that live in Time and apply them when you're back," his father told him. Tom nodded and left the kitchen. On his way out he passed the living room where he saw the treadmill where his dad was currently running. He walked out of the house where he looked right and left down the hallway. He started walking towards the center of the Community Center. He knew where he needed to be.

Chapter X

Through the Corridor

Tom sat in the beautiful green grass staring at his ballot. The rectangular piece of paper outstretched in front of him along the grass. His focus wasn't on the greenery, the trees surrounding the park, or the people sitting around watching as their loved ones entered through the curtain. No, Tom was solely focused on the small rectangular ballot laying quietly in front of him. Tom attempted to find the connection between the ballot and the blurry curtain far in the distance down the hill. Occasionally, he would notice the curtain a little more and it would come into focus. It ominously hung in the center of the park only a short walk away.

Tom waited. He didn't know exactly why he waited. He only knew this was where he was supposed to be. He didn't know how to get to the second floor, but he also knew he didn't have to know. When the time came, his path would come to him. Just as he met Eric and the same way he met his parents; he would soon see exactly why he was in this place and questioned the ballot in front of him.

The ballot was something Tom had many misunderstandings about in correlation with the curtain. He wanted to know more about the so-called inherent connection between it and the curtain. He didn't understand why people put seemingly all their beliefs into this small rectangular shaped paper. On the front there were the average religions most people subscribed to. His mother and Eric fell into these beliefs. As one read down the list, one would be greeted by different religions not as many people believed in, but some did. He wondered what made the religions at the bottom any less viable than the ones near the top. More people certainly believed in the ones at the top. But was that only it? Was the popularity of a certain belief what made it any truer? As if truth was on a scale and one could move closer to it instead of just knowing the truth. But what information did the religions at the top hold that suggested their truth was any more viable than let's say "the flying spaghetti monster". A silly sounding religion. But there it is, closer to the bottom of the ballot. It can't be the right belief to choose, of course. But why "of course"? Did Tom's Christianity hold any more truth than the flying spaghetti monster? Or maybe his mother was right. Maybe it didn't matter what belief was right or wrong but only what you believe in.

As Tom looked at his ballot and once again glanced at the curtain beyond, he couldn't help but think everyone believing in these religions were all on the same side of the curtain. Even his mother's explanation was on this side of the curtain. Everyone only taking stabs into complete darkness as to what was beyond the curtain. How is it so farfetched to say Christianity was built as a structure for humanity to have morals? Its only purpose was to manipulate a people who were evil into obeying lists of rules as best they could. And equally as viable, how is it so farfetched that a noodle god created everything? Tom didn't like any of these ideas but for whatever reason he couldn't escape them. He didn't like thinking he could be an atheist. But Tom simply didn't know and more importantly, Tom didn't understand how anyone *could* know.

Tom picked up his ballot and looked at the letters written out more carefully. He read the various religions and all their different meanings. At the top of the ballot in smaller font was a short sentence that annoyed Tom. "Beliefs are subject to change based on who you speak to". Tom rolled his eyes and flicked the ballot away from him landing softly on the grass. What was the point of the ballot at all then? If everything is subject to change based on who he speaks with then the ballot is completely useless to him. It only strengthened his idea that no one actually knows anything at all.

He glanced around the park looking at people. The

ranges of emotion as people walked through the curtain varied wildly. Some were laughing, some cried, a couple people were hitting the grass with their fists in anger, and some people just spoke quietly to one another. And all of them sat quietly with their own beliefs and religions hoping they chose the right answer on their ballot. They all hoped their loved ones went on to a better place based on the vote they gave on a ballot... a ballot made by people. Although Tom was told about the division in the Community Center, he saw everyone in the park the same. He couldn't tell if someone was from Phestiles or from Acedia. Not that Tom would recognize anyone from Phestiles, the division of the Community Center he'd never seen. But he knew they were there in the park also. They too mourned the loss of their loved ones.

Tom first felt the persons presence. Then, he looked down and saw a knee that was probably mirrored on the other side in a cross-legged fashion similar to the way Tom sat. The persons knee was covered by a brown pant. The man wore a suit jacket with a nice vest underneath. A tie was nicely wrapped around his neck hoisting a large head. He was older and resembled that of a professor of some sort. He had lines stretching from the sides of his nose past his mouth fading off his chin. His eyes were curious as they looked at Tom and the ballot he just flicked. Tom didn't think the man's eyes were necessarily old and wise, they only looked curious and somewhat funny. He had a bald head but apparently the sides didn't get the memo, so they continued to grow. The man was seated next to Tom in a way suggesting he was meant to sit there. Tom immediately knew this was where he was supposed to be. And now you know, how I stopped Clive from walking through the curtain.

"I'm terribly sorry for your loss," Clive said. Tom was confused why this strange man was speaking to him in the first place but was not oppose to the idea of meeting him. You might be thinking to yourself that Clive is clearly the person meant to take Tom to the second floor. And why doesn't Tom know this inherently? He knew he was supposed to meet someone. So why doesn't he assume it's this man? Because Tom doesn't know that anymore. He knew that before Clive appeared. But he doesn't know that anymore. Now Tom only knew that he was sitting in the grass looking at his ballot and the curtain. Meeting this man is a surprise to him. Welcome to the Community Center, where time doesn't work the way you know.

"I haven't lost anyone," Tom said to the strange man who looked straight forward at the curtain. A few people entered every few moments and wails of cries were heard echoing throughout the park.

"I'm not speaking about the curtain," Clive told him. Tom leaned forward, picked up his ballot, and looked at it confused.

"Because I'm lost in knowing what to believe," Tom said concluding the man's thoughts, a little disappointed. Not disappointment in what the man said but disappointed in not knowing what to believe.

"Not that either. But because you believe that you *are* lost," Clive smiled and let out a small laugh. The comment Clive made to Tom was ironic to him as he was actually there to end his own existence. But now that he was speaking to someone who struggled with thoughts just as his own, he could argue from another perspective. Tom was of course lost to the irony but deeply enjoyed the carefree nature about the man.

"But if I'm not lost then what am I?" Tom asked. Clive stood up from his spot and started to walk away back through the entrance Tom came from, the division of the Community Center, Acedia. Tom turned around and quickly jumped up to follow the strange and curious man.

"You're seeking my boy," Clive said putting his hands into his pocket. He felt the puzzle piece he hung onto for most his existence. Tom did seek and he knew this. But the purpose of seeking was to find, right?

"Who are you?" Tom asked as he followed the man up the hill and back into the corridor. Clive didn't answer at first. He only thought about the entangled predicament he was now in with this young man. He thought about how simple something as meeting someone new made him forget about the questions he had and his intent on going through the curtain. It no longer mattered whether or not Clive had free will.

The two men made it to a food court and sat down at a table. Acedia was as relaxed as every as Clive looked around. Various people went about their days and Clive quietly people watched. Tom only could think about what the man meant when he said "seeking". He could only think about what belief he should be a part of on his own ballot. He put the ballot down on the table and continued to stare at it as Clive watched different people all with their own stories to tell.

"My name is Clive. What's yours?" the silence was finally broken. If Tom were to look closer at Clive he would see he wasn't just watching individual people. He was searching for someone specific as they both sat at the table.

"Thomas... Tom," he replied. Clive smiled but didn't stop looking for the person of interest to him. Suddenly, his eyes locked on the person. In the distance, Clive saw an elderly man weaving in and out of crowds. Tom looked down at his ballot ignoring whatever it was Clive was watching. He thought maybe older people had inside knowledge to what any of existence was actually about or maybe answers to the curtain.

"Do you believe 'beliefs' are important?" Tom asked. Clive continued to concentrate on the elderly man in the distance he recognized. The man would disappear for a few moments behind trash cans and people only to reappear suddenly.

"The ballot? Most forget about it when they enter existence. Other than the weekly cycle of practicing the religion you marked," Clive replied still watching the decrepit elderly man in the distance. He was mostly unseen by the people wandering around the shops. He would slip behind various corridors and counters reappearing on the other side of a completely different shop. It almost looked like a magic trick to the untrained eye. Occasionally, he would stop one of the people walking around different shops. He would whisper something and hand them something small. He would then jump joyously in the air and run away. The people had different reactions to the man but mostly were confused by what they were handed. But all of them quietly and politely put the object in their pocket and continued about their day. He was a man only noticed by the ones he gave the object to, and those who would pause to look for him.

"So, you don't think they're important then?" Tom asked. He was unnoticing of the elderly man Clive watched.

"The question itself is interesting in essence. But so is seeking I suppose," Clive said.

"How so?" Tom asked.

"You're asking if I *believe* if beliefs are important or not. The nature of the question implies there isn't a way to *know*. You didn't ask me if I *knew* beliefs were important. If you did, then you would be open to the idea that we can know something to be absolute. But you didn't. So, your preconception of any answer I give is already that there is no possible way for me to have an answer for you," Clive said continuing to watch the man. Tom tried to follow as much as he could without coming off ignorant. He could tell Clive was much smarter than he was.

"Then... do you *know* beliefs are important?" Tom asked feeling a little foolish. Yet, he didn't know why. But Clive's face showed a perseverance with no intention to waver from the conversation.

"A simple turn of phrase to get you on the right path. I like that," Clive replied smiling slightly thinking again of the irony. The irony that a simple change in the world seemed to have also put Clive back on the right path. "Do you know the man over there?" Clive asked. Tom didn't feel as though the man was ignoring his question but felt as though this was part of the answer.

Looking to the shops Tom squinted his eyes. There were many different people in the crowds. He saw a tall man passing money to a shorter man in exchange for a product. He saw some men walking with women who could easily be friends or lovers. He saw some men laughing together as they shared drinks on bar stools. But he did see one specific man who stood out once he found him. The elderly stranger with a crooked back and crazed look. Someone Tom had encountered once before. Tom watched as the man darted back and forth between men and women who ignored his existence. Or was it possible that it was the elderly man who ignored their existence?

Tom reached into his pocket and pulled out the puzzle piece he was given earlier. He placed it at the top of the ballot in front of Clive. "I know him. He gave me this," Tom explained. Reaching into his own pocket, Clive pulled out his puzzle piece and placed it on the table. The two pieces were clearly quite different and didn't even look as though they belonged to the same puzzle. Clive's piece was bright and colorful. It was weirdly shaped with sharp edges.

"He gave you one also?" Tom asked.

"He gives most people a piece," Clive told Tom as he looked at them both on the table.

"Why?" Tom asked after a moment of silence. Clive sighed.

"Why, indeed. You didn't know the man. He didn't know you. I was the first he gave the piece to as he told me it was what I would hinge every decision I ever make on. I didn't know what he meant really. But I've kept it ever since," Clive said.

"Who is he?" Tom asked, he could see in Clive's eyes that he knew the man.

"He was my teacher. He was my mentor for many years. Until the questions drove him to what you see there," Clive continued as he suddenly gestured to the man. "What do you suppose his beliefs are? And why do you think he is so old yet none the wiser? When he was my teacher he showed me how to question. But what do you think he believes?" Clive asked.

Tom didn't have an answer. He had no answer for existence, beliefs, or for the man giving away strange puzzle pieces. He sat trying to sift through the information in his head but was coming up with nothing. The spotlight shown on Tom from Clive created anxiety. Tom's mind was blank until he looked back to the elderly stranger.

"What made him like that?" Tom finally asked Clive.

"Something evil. Something plaguing all of us but

took a darker toll on him," Clive said. The term "evil" was foreign to Tom. He didn't think much on it though. He was only curious about the elderly man.

"Can we follow him? I want to know about him," Tom asked staring at the stranger. Suddenly he disappeared into a dark corridor no others were walking into. The slender corridor was unnoticed until the man went down it. Clive turned to Tom with a smile on his face.

"Ah, a man looking for answers. Not lost. But someone who seeks," Clive said. Collecting his puzzle piece and ballot, Tom stood up and walked towards the dark corridor with Clive. Standing at its entrance, they could see small flickering florescent lights, trash spread everywhere, and their noses were hit with a raw stench. Tom scrunched his face but paid no attention as he wanted to know where the hallway led. But even more, he wanted to know why the elderly stranger gave him a puzzle piece to begin with.

The two men entered the corridor. As they did, graffiti came into view written across the wall. Unlike the graffiti near the curtain, these were full of profanity and anger. It didn't scare Tom, because he knew everything here existed under the same umbrella as everything else. Clive was quickly reminded of Phestiles and the anger of its citizens. How it slowly would grow into this place and eventually take the entire Community Center. This did worry Clive, but saw how much Tom wanted to understand existence. The only thing striking fear into Tom's heart was whatever was beyond the curtain. The unknown not held under the umbrella of existence.

"No peace... no peace...," a whisper echoed through the corridor. Tom and Clive paused at the ominous atmosphere. But Tom didn't hear it as a piece of the puzzle this time. It was a cry for help from someone who would never know peace. There would never be any calm. There would only be chaos. As they turned a corner, they saw the elderly stranger with his knees bent to the ground. His hands were clasped, and he looked at something exceptionally large on the wall in front of him. It was a puzzle. A large blank puzzle placed vertically on the wall like a painting. Large lights powered by generators sat to either side and illuminated it creating a brilliant altar. Directly in the center of the puzzle was one single missing piece. Tom immediately pulled out his own piece and held it up as he walked slowly to the wall. The elderly man paid no attention, he only worshiped the large puzzle. Tom could see the puzzle was infatuating, but Tom was also very aware of it being infatuating. Clive stood still as Tom studied the aspects of the scene in front of him.

"What is it?" Tom asked. Clive walked slowly to where Tom now stood.

"To me?" Clive sighed. "It's a reminder of what would happen if I stared at the curtain too long," Clive said. Tom looked back at him and could see Clive had seen this place before. "I was like you Tom. He was like you," Clive said gesturing to the man. "We too sat in the park always staring at the curtain. For days on end until people forgot about us. We tried finding answers by defeating the great evil that plagues the first floor. We found it. And we came back even more empty handed than before...." Clive continued. There was that word "evil" again. But he didn't care for it. He didn't even have an interest in it. "...I've wanted so long to know what's beyond the curtain that I feel I will just walk through out of curiosity one day. After I returned from meeting evil. I found my professor again. But I found him like this. He didn't know me anymore. He only cared about his puzzle. It's when he gave me the puzzle piece. I thought I could complete the picture and that's why he gave it to me. But... you'll see...." Clive reached in his pocket and pulled out his piece holding it up. "...You'll see no piece fits the puzzle."

Here Tom realized what the puzzle was and what it meant. The elderly stranger stressed every day and night over the puzzle. Tom walked closer to the man worshiping it and placed his hand on his shoulder. The elderly man only kept repeating the same thing over and over.

"No peace... no peace...," the whispers echoed as he clasped his hands together to worship his own misunderstandings.

Looking closer, Tom could see the man's eyes were filled with tears. It was as if he were trapped in his own thoughts and had no escape other than to fill the missing piece. Tom placed his own puzzle piece on the ground in front of the elderly man and walked back to Clive.

"You asked me if I know beliefs are important. They are. Beliefs allow questions to fade away long enough for us to live," Clive said as he clutched onto his puzzle piece and returned it to his pocket. Tom didn't like this answer. He felt as though this was only a way to distract him from the absolute truth. But looking back to the puzzle on the wall, he could see the elderly man was the one distracted.

"Out in the Community Center where we have this useless ballot...," Clive said as he took his own ballot out. "We all have a singular belief we suspect has influence over what is after the curtain. But belief in any of these puzzle pieces has no affect on the puzzle itself. Truth requires belief as much as air requires our breath. It doesn't," Clive said turning around and walking back outside the corridor. He paused for a moment and turned back. "The man in there is lost. I am lost. You are seeking Tom. Do not lose yourself as you seek."

Tom stood in silence for a moment. He looked back at the elderly man who became obsessed with the unknown. He was engulfed with questions where he was now distracted from the life happening only a walk away. Tom joined Clive and they both walked outside into the bustling of life. Deep beneath the surface of Tom's thoughts another contradiction grew. Tom thought to himself that the curtain required existence. Truth didn't require belief, but the curtain required someone to exist for it to be used. Now, an interesting conundrum, did existence require the curtain?

"I need to go to the second floor," Tom said as they

both exited the corridor. Clive stopped but kept looking around at the people in the cafeteria they once sat in.

"Not surprising. Someone who seeks will eventually find themselves in its labyrinth," Clive said calmly.

"So, it's a labyrinth?" Tom asked excitedly.

"One has never been so lost than in the straight labyrinth of Time. I'll take you there on one condition...," Clive told Tom with a pause. "You will go with me to meet evil," he concluded. Tom had no objection to this as he didn't know what evil necessarily was. He only nodded his head. Clive, on the other hand, wanted to see if Tom could possibly be the one to finally rid the first floor of evil.

Chapter XI

An Atheist and a Christian

Grab a drink with your friends because Tom has found his goal! He wishes to discover more information about existence through what the second floor can offer. Up there, Tom was told Time can give him what he needs. Which hasn't really been discussed between you and I yet. How is he not already experiencing Time if he is in one place and will experience something else in a moment? That, in itself, is a measurement of time, right? Even if this book is written non-linear and we see Tom knows things before they happen it is still a measurement of time by the readers standards. Simply put, non-linear time is still time. The only difference is it seems to be jumbled up between past, present, and future. Sometimes two time periods (like the present and past) are happening at the same time as we've seen before. If this is true, then the second floor would only be an organized timeline to view.

So, how is it that Tom and the citizens of the Community Center are actually outside of time? Maybe they are or maybe they only believe they are based on their perception. The only way to find out would be to follow Tom to the second floor. That isn't meant to be a terrible cash grab to get you to keep reading. Unfortunately, it's something you'll understand (at least a little better) once Tom reaches the second floor. At which point you will be caught up to the point where he is... now? I think? Time is a funny thing. I think that's right.

Yes, it is. Afterwards we can discuss the deliciousness of the sandwich and what type of character Tom is at that point in time. Or feel free to skip ahead to the last chapter when it's all caught up. You'll recognize some things and some things you won't. You'll understand Tom does go behind the curtain and that you as the reader find out what is behind it.

Oops. Was that a spoiler? Sometimes I think you already know these things but have to remember you see time linear. Forget I said anything about Tom going behind the curtain. Let's only focus on where he is right now and when he goes to the second floor.

Tom and Clive are walking through... great. Now it's stuck in my head also. And I already know the ending of this book too! I'm there right now and also at the beginning of this book! It's very difficult to concentrate when they're all happening at once and you want me to stay right here.

Let's move to someone else then. Maybe that will help. I think we've seen enough of Tom for another chapter anyway. Ah, there she is. Right now, there's a woman speaking in front of a crowd in Acedia. Not far from where Tom is currently walking, but this chapter is about her and what she wants out of existence.

"How quickly people use their faith as a reason to believe but shy away when they're asked to use it for any other purpose," the young woman says, finishing her speech to the crowd. Around ten to fifteen people stand around her as she stands on a chair telling them her thoughts. A small beany sits upside down in front of her with wadded up money. The crowd seems somewhat interested, with only a few people walking away and some still coming up to her. She thinks about all the most popular Christian speakers and how much money they raise for their churches, yet very few people give to her because she doesn't preach the cookie cutter words. She was raised Christian but wouldn't deny that she often wondered if she should change her answer to possibly agnostic. She didn't get much support from her fellow Christians anyway. And, after all, she would conclude that she never truly knew what was real and what wasn't real. But we already spoke about those questions when we followed Tom.

She existed for a little bit longer than Tom but not by much. Probably about a month or two now but arrived at the same time he did. She enjoyed the narrative of Christianity and felt it was probably as close as any to knowing what was after the curtain. So, she took it upon herself to question things within the narrative of her religion. Her very first question was a pretty obvious one, "Is there a God?" It's a question even the most deeply faithful have. Being faithful has never meant not having questions, it's only ever been the evidence when there is no answer to your questions. Since she was unable to find absolute answers to questions like this, she dug deeper into maybe ignored flaws of Christianity. Recently, she asked herself about faith and why she had it. What purpose did it serve other than to create a stalemate with an atheist? You know exactly what she's talking about if you're a devout Christian. If a religious person argues with an atheist, the argument will most likely end with the religious person saying something about beliefs coming down to faith. The religious person sees this as a checkmate and the atheist sees this as a cheap ploy to end the discussion. Our new friend (Kate by the way) hated seeing this. She didn't think faith should be reduced to just the ending of a debate. Faith is defined as proof of things not yet seen. It must have had much more potential than just to win arguments with people who didn't believe.

She reached in her pocket and held onto a small puzzle piece she carried with her since she arrived in the Community Center. The people started to disperse from the area as she stepped off the stool. She picked up her beanie, took the money out, and put her beanie back on. Speaking in front of crowds as she did was a common practice in the Community Center. When someone had an idea or interesting thoughts they wanted to share, they would promptly stand in front of everyone who was willing to listen. Most people would go most their existence never even stepping on a stool. But for those confident in what they had to say, it was very normal. Kate had many ideas she wanted to share. She typically spoke in the same four areas of Acedia as she saw it's where the wealthy gave more. Every so often one of the men or women would come to her afterwards and tell her they enjoyed listening. But no one ever seemed to want to engage in what she said with a different view. It was as if her preaching turned into a slice of deep-thinking people could chew on through their week, but nothing more. She was gum. She was something easily disposed of between meals, but the real consumption began with peoples personal relationships and lives. She was only there to make people think and not act.

She didn't like being gum. But I don't think anyone wants to be gum. She started to walk away down a hall counting the money given until she bumped into someone. Thinking it was simply a mistake she started to move out of the way, but she looked up and saw a young woman not moving out of her way.

"Faith is the bridge between where I am and where God wants me to be," the young woman told her. Kate could see the gleam of ignorance radiating from this woman's eyes. The young girl didn't look like anyone who'd ever ventured more than twenty-five yards from her section in the Community Center. Kate gritted her teeth because of the definition the young woman gave.

Even though it was innocently given, Kate had a difficult time speaking with people who lived their lives through inspirational quotes.

Kate nodded her head politely and walked away from the young woman. She put her back against an empty wall taking a deep breath. Kate knew what faith was and didn't doubt what the woman said to be true. Her argument wasn't about what faith *is*, her argument was about whether or not people are using the bridge or not. Were people just pointing across the bridge to an atheist and saying "See that way over there? That's God. I know it's him because of this beautiful bridge I have."

Was faith only being used as a means to try and rectify this pain of not having answers? Or was it being used to walk across the bridge? Kate thought many people watch the bridge, many people constantly talk about the bridge, but few ever walk across it. Do everyday people even know how to walk across it? Do you have to be completely enlightened or have your doctorate in theology to understand how to walk across it? Kate remembered seeing people pray over a blind person and when they weren't healed she would hear those same people say, "We must have not had enough faith." As if faith is the bar we're trying to reach and not the ladder we should use to climb. Is faith only the magical elixir we need enough of so God will be satisfied enough to heal someone?

She pulled out the puzzle piece in her pocket. It had a black circle in the middle and was not a corner piece. She knew what it was. She'd followed the elderly stranger just as Tom did. But she held onto her piece. Like most do, she wanted her piece to fit the puzzle of life. But she knew it never would. Christianity wasn't the answer to whatever was behind the curtain. She only hoped God was. She held it close to her chest.

She was so frustrated over the intricacies of her own religion and the fact no one did anything to gain answers. It was as if everyone wanted answers just to make the questions go away, but no one wanted the actual answers. People flocked to whatever spiritual awakening they could obtain but gave no thought to God. They looked for answers that would neatly check the boxes off but didn't look for *the* answer. Did you find your spiritual awakening standing in the pew of a church? Maybe you found your enlightenment from a bad trip on mushrooms as you thought deeply about multidimensional travels. Your journey may have taken you to a homeless shelter to help others. But nothing stopped Kate from thinking these all occurred under the same roof as everything else. What was beyond though?

"I liked your speech," a man said to her as she thought heavily. She held onto her puzzle piece and cash tightly. She looked up and saw Eric. Someone she didn't know yet but was starting to slowly recognize. Kate looked around a little suspicious of Eric.

"Who knew you could swindle so much money from people just by talking," he concluded sarcastically. This rude comment forced her to sigh. She put the money in her pocket and started to walk away. Eric followed close behind her.

"You're not usually the type to listen. Are you Christian?" she asked him. He laughed.

"No, I'm not. I'm an atheist. I'm Eric," he said putting his hand out to shake hers as they walked.

"I know, we've met before but I'm not there yet," she said shaking his hand. She wasn't interested in defending her religion or spiritual journey to an atheist.

"Don't worry. I'm not into conversion. But I do like any speech that points out flaws in religion," he said to her as if they were on the same page.

"The flaws I point out aren't to dis-sway anyone from Christianity. It's only to make people think about and hopefully find answers to the questions in the religion," she explained to him defensively. Eric thought about it for a moment.

"Don't act high and mighty when you just pocketed money from people," he told her. She went quiet. This hurt her slightly. Eric didn't know her and didn't know what she was doing. She stopped in front of a small kitchen window where a large dirty man stood with a ladle. Eric looked around the edge of the window for any sign for what it was. There was no sign, there were no other shops in the hallway they were in. It was a little bit of a dirty area to be in.

"Hey Kate, it's nice to see you again. How the speeches?" the man behind the window asked Kate. She smiled and put her hands on the counter to look inside the small opening.

"It's running wild like always. How's mama?" she asked the man. He sniffed and gargled something in his throat.

"It's been tough since Lady went behind the curtain. But... you know how it goes. She's a fighter," he said. His voice booming with every word. Eric looked left and right awkwardly. He couldn't see a menu to order lunch or anything at all. He didn't really see the purpose of the kitchen and ignored the inside pleasantries Kate and the man shared.

"I'm really sorry to hear about Lady. If I see her then I'll let her know you miss her," Kate replied. She reached into her pocket and pulled out the money that was given to her. She placed it on the counter. The man reached out and picked it up sliding it into an envelope.

"Thanks Kate. This will help a lot. You let me know if there's anything I can do to keep those speeches going," he smiled at her. She smiled back and said goodbye walking away.

Eric immediately realized the kitchen was for homeless people down on their luck and needing a warm meal. "Atheists help people too. It's not exclusive to Christianity," he told her as they walked.

"I didn't say they didn't or that it was?" she replied confused. She didn't care either. She never once thought about whether atheists help or not. She only ever thought about what she could do to help others.

"I'm just saying there's some bad Christians and there's some bad atheists. People are just bad or good no matter what they believe," Eric explained to her.

She kept walking, uncaring of his ego.

"What do you want Eric?" she asked him. He smiled.

"You know we're actually friends?" Eric said. Kate knew it was possible but didn't care to really think about it deeply. She didn't recall being friends with someone as fragile as Eric clearly was. "We're friends because of Tom," he continued.

"You know Tom? Thomas Lewis?" she exclaimed suddenly.

"Oh yeah, we go way back. He was born just the other day,"

"I haven't met him yet. But he's my husband," she said to him. Eric wasn't fazed by this as he already knew Kate and Tom were married. He had seen it before and knew a little more than she did at this moment.

"I know. I know you haven't met him yet. Fair warning, he's different," he told her as they walked. She lowered her head, a little disappointed at what she heard.

"Why do you say that? What's wrong with him?" her tone of voice picked up as she switched from being disappointed, to being a little offended at the accusatory remark at her husband. Even though, she hadn't even met him yet.

"For starters, he doesn't shut up about beliefs...," Eric explained. She grinned as she walked. She wanted someone who questioned things intently. "...but most of all he doesn't shut up about the curtain. He is extremely interested in the curtain for whatever reason," he said as he motioned his hands. Kate stopped in the middle of the hallway.

"Why does he talk a lot about the curtain?" she asked him. Eric stopped; he could see something was stirring in her head. A memory was forming in front of him.

"He saw a suicide when he stepped off the bus," Eric said. And like a dam breaking, tears rained down her face. Something snapped inside her head and her arms began to tremor. Eric grabbed her to keep her from falling down. He didn't understand what was happening because he had no knowledge of this part in Tom and Kates lives. But she was just reminded of something involving her husband. Something tragic Tom didn't know about yet.

Sitting down on the floor, Kate pushed herself against the wall. Eric sat next to her in silence trying to only be there for his friend. Her breath was heavy. She tried not to think of whatever memory she had just encountered.

"Where is he now?" she asked. Eric knew Tom met with his parents and went to the second floor with Clive.

"He should be coming back from the second floor," Eric told her. She gasped at what she heard and a few more tears fell. Eric could see the confusion, hatred, and bewilderment in her eyes.

"Time isn't as scary as they say it is. He wanted to see why the man committed suicide. He wanted answers," he told her trying to comfort her. But he only made it worse.

"I could've told him," she said under her breath.

This statement confused Eric. But it was interrupted by a surprising voice standing only feet away from them.

"Kate...," the voice said. Looking up, Kate saw her husband standing in the hallway. Tom held something tight in his right hand, but she didn't know what it was. She had never seen it before. Eric's mouth gaped open at the object in his hand. He knew what it was and more importantly knew Tom wasn't supposed to have it.

Chapter XII

From Eternity to the Beginning

Tom has only been a "point of view" character for us to see into this strange world called the Community Center. From the moment Tom woke on the bus to be greeted in this fantastical yet mysterious place, to where he is right now; Tom has only been a vessel for the reader to project and see from his lens. But have we ever met Tom? I don't think we have. We know descriptions about him. We know he desperately wants to know what's beyond the curtain, and that he wants to know why someone killed themselves. But we've only seen what his soul experienced in waiting to walk through the curtain. A sort of purgatory of not understanding anything other than what other souls tell him about existence. Imagine, living in a place where the only beings you can trust are ones who know nothing more than you. *Wink wink.*

But there he is, our protagonist Tom. Now beyond the curtain and in full knowledge of what he's always wanted to know. In other words (and words Tom only learned recently), he died. You didn't read that incorrectly. You haven't skipped too far ahead in the book. Our main character died. And when Tom died an overwhelming understanding of who he was in existence flooded his mind where he no longer cared about the curtain.

But that didn't happen only beyond the curtain, his understanding of Time and the curtain happened right now when he was in it's presence on the second floor. A singular moment of tragedy was all it took to propel Tom from the place in his chair where he ate a sandwich, to beyond death. Yes, the very sandwich I spoke about in the first chapter of this book. It's the very sandwich he's been looking at the entire book because it's the sandwich that takes his life from him.

It was a simple but beautifully crafted sandwich. It was two slices of white bread, honey ham, mustard, and crushed potato chips to add a level of texture. A tear rolled down his face reflecting from the florescent lights shining brightly as he stared at the sandwich. It sat on a circular white plate with a glass of water next to it. Not a soul hustled around the food court as they were all asleep during the busiest time of day. But this didn't bother Tom, nor did he dwell on the idea of Time and its effects on the first floor. Tom's parents were probably at their home fast asleep. Kate was just about to arrive in the Community Center. Eric had passed behind the curtain years prior.

Tom sat in his chair remembering the last conversation he had with Kate and Eric. His wife was in a state of panic and anxiety as she couldn't find the goodness left in the world. Tom gave his empty promises to her in order to find anything in the Community Center which was good. But you're not aware of this journey Tom takes yet. You're not aware of the toll it takes on his friends and family. We haven't even made it to the second floor and now I'm talking about Tom's last moments. In his last moments he reflected meaningful words to himself. The words would remind him every day that time does not operate the same on the first floor as it does on the second. A sign of hope for Tom. It all made sense to Tom even if it didn't to you. He knew his wife years prior to ever meeting her. She never arrived on the bus as he did but would soon begin her existence long before she ever ended it. Experiencing Time on the second floor was something that shifted how Tom viewed existence.

The elevator doors opened and revealed a small enclosure. Red carpet lined the walls with golden designs. Warm lights illuminated the room and a ding alerted Tom he needed to step into the elevator. Tom turned around and looked at Clive as he entered the warm lights. He didn't say anything and neither did Clive. They quietly nodded to each other and grinned slightly. Clive portrayed such intelligence, but his eyes were wondrous and curious. Tom looked to his right and saw two very clean buttons. One of them labelled 1 and the other 2. Tom pressed the button for the second floor, the doors slid closed, and Clive disappeared.

Tom's stomach sank as he felt himself being lifted. He looked at his reflection in the clean metal. He thought he was slowly beginning to resemble the crazed eyes of the elderly stranger with the puzzle pieces. He reached into his pocket and felt it's emptiness. Tom gave up his puzzle piece. He was a blank slate who didn't want to *believe* in anything but only wanted to *know*. Who knows, maybe the second floor would give Tom the answers to his questioning.

The bell in the elevator rang disrupting his thoughts. It's doors slid open. What Tom saw next was something no soul knew how to fully express into words. On the other hand, I do. Because it's something you (the reader of this book) will understand much more than Tom did. It was where time operated linearly, and things happened one after the other. Confused, Tom didn't see anything too unusual yet. He saw a dark wooden floor stretching to meet a podium. A man sat behind the podium looking down at something. Behind the man and podium there was only perceived darkness. The walls to the left and right were beautiful stone with dimly lit candles every few feet to barely illuminate the dark.

Tom stepped onto the wood almost expecting something otherworldly to happen. But nothing did. He simply stepped forward. As Tom continued, the man sitting at the podium came closer into view. He had white hair and wore small glasses on the edge of his nose. Wrinkles filled his face, but he was a man who looked as though he should be old. You know the type, those elderly people you could never imagine being any younger than one hundred years old. The man wore a well-fitted vest and bowtie matching the warm atmosphere of the room. As Tom slowly walked closer, he could see the man's eyes were studying something on the podium but he couldn't tell what it was.

The man seemed to ignore Tom or didn't see him walking up to the podium. Tom looked at his hands and stretched his fingers. He lifted his legs high and then put them down stretching out his body humorously. Tom attempted to see if he felt any different than when he was on the first floor. He didn't. He felt exactly the same. Tom thought he might experience a psychedelic hallucination, or something drug related. Instead, he stood in the middle of a nice hallway with a man and his podium. Sure, it was a nice hallway, but it wasn't like Tom hadn't seen nice hallways on the first floor. Tom walked closer to the podium which now towered over him a full foot. He could barely see the elderly man high above him now. Tom gave a half-cough to alert the man to his presence. Slowly, the man looked away from whatever was on the podium, leaned forward, and looked at Tom annoyed that his attention was distracted.

"How can I help you today, Tom?" the man rolled his eyes feeling dull. Swallowing slightly, and puzzled by the man's reaction, Tom quietly answered.

"Um... I'm looking to find out what happened to David," he said. The man sighed and grasped the edge of the podium with his hand. Tom heard a loud thump on the podium as the man hopped down from his chair to meet Tom's eyeline. Actually, his chest, the man was very short.

"I know. But just as I've told you before, I don't know how to help you without a last name," the man told Tom. With this comment, Tom knew who he was. The man called himself the Captain and Tom had met with him several times before. The Captains job was in the keeping of Time. Tom now understood the second floor held Time; it wasn't Time itself.

The Captain continued to stare at Tom who now understand this wasn't the first time he'd been to the second floor. All the moments before, Tom would ask if he could see David and every time the Captain turned Tom away. You see, unlike the first floor, Time holds every David to exist from the beginning to the end. Without a last name there was very little the Captain could help with. Tom was never able to truly experience Time because the Captain had nothing to show him.

Tom thought to himself for a moment. This moment had to be different than all the times before. Afterall, Tom was experiencing this moment instead of only remembering it. There was something different for Tom to discover here. The Captain started to climb back up on his chair to continue whatever it was he was doing.

"When you find a name then come get...," the

Captain started to say.

"What about my name? What can you tell me about Thomas Lewis?" he asked the Captain who stopped mid-climb. A grin split across his face. He turned to look at Tom as if he'd cracked the code.

"Ah! Now that is the right question. Certainly, I can help you with that," the Captain said almost with a jump. The Captain showed exceptional excitement for Tom. Out of all the moments he'd met Tom, this was the one where Tom would finally understand Time.

"Follow me!" the Captain said as he picked up a lantern from his podium. Tom glanced around for a moment and followed him into the darkness. Looking back at the podium, Tom glanced at what the Captain was doing. Sitting on the podium was the work the Captain attended to when he walked in but couldn't make out exactly what it was.

As the darkness consumed them both the lantern light did nothing more than to illuminate their own selves. Only a few inches of the lanterns soft glow of light allowed the Captain to see where he walked. He stopped abruptly and fumbled to touch the wall. Tom heard a click, and suddenly a large room was brightly lit. Large lanterns of brilliant flame ignited around the enormous circular room. It was by far the largest room Tom had ever seen as it stretched far into the distance. The switch ignited the flames standing on large pillars. The room was much lower than the two men currently. Stairs directly in front of them led to large columns in the center of the room. From the top,

Tom thought it resembled Clive's analogy of a labyrinth with many different hallways. Although enormous in size, the room felt warm and kind. It was welcoming and simply beautiful. Tom and the Captain started to walk down the steps to the large columns. The steps leading down were covered in a soft red-carpet. Time was especially nice to look at.

"Do you go through the curtain eventually too?" Tom asked the Captain who waltzed down the stairs casually. He stopped for a moment to try and answer Tom's inquiry.

"What kind of question is that?" he asked after a moment of confusion.

"I mean, you're up here away from the Community Center. Stands to reason you're not in existence. Just a question," Tom shrugged as he looked at the confused old man.

"Just because I'm up here doesn't mean I don't exist, Tom," he turned around and began walking down the steps again. "Just because Time is separate from you doesn't mean it doesn't exist either. Some would argue it exists even *more* than we do," the Captain continued. This really puzzled Tom.

"Are you saying Time will go behind the curtain one day too? Is nothing safe from the curtain?" Tom asked, now unsure of a lot of things. The old Captain started to walk again grinning at Tom's questions. It was a sense of joy for the Captain, knowing Tom's confusion came from a place of genuine curiosity and not a place of manipulation.

"Oh, Tom. You misunderstand what Time is. But I guess most do on the first floor," he said as they reached the bottom of the stairs. They were now level with the large columns towering over them. Large constructs holding strange and colorful rectangles.

"Time exists yet it only exists when it is observed. Any moment a person stops observing Time it ceases to be, and the moment we look back to Time it surprises us once again," the Captain continued. This really confused Tom. "You also seem to think things only exist if they go through the curtain. As if the curtain gives us existence," he continued.

"But the curtain is what gives existence meaning?" Tom told the Captain.

"The curtain gives existence meaning as much as an empty glass of water gives meaning to a full glass of water. The meaning doesn't come from the act of going through the curtain but the acts it can do for others," the Captain explained. Instead of trying to debate and answer, Tom only wanted to experience Time for himself.

He followed the Captain past large shelves full of different colors separated neatly. Tom wondered if this had anything to do with Time. Each of these hallways had a large ladder reaching to the top shelf on either side. The hallways were long and felt never-ending. Looking closely at the various colors he could see names swirled in design written on them. The different colors ranged in size before they bled into the next. Some colors were small, and some colors were large, but they all sat neatly next to one another. Tom was very confused as to what they were.

As they walked, the Captain grabbed a ladder on one specific hallway and slid it down the aisle stopping abruptly. He climbed up a quarter of the way and pulled a color off the shelf. From what Tom could see, the color was solid and firm in the Captains hand. He climbed down the ladder and gave it to Tom.

Tom held it. It was heavier than he expected. It wasn't the thickest rectangle of color he saw on the shelf, but it wasn't terribly small. The front was red leather with an embroidery reading his own name. It didn't feel old or worn, in fact it felt very new. It was something Tom had never seen before and didn't understand how to use. He knew it felt warm and inviting which was a nice contrast to the first floor.

"This... Tom... is a book. It's something you've never encountered before. I can't explain what Time is, but you will understand it once you open it up and begin to read," the Captain explained. Tom glanced at all the other books surrounding him and saw they were much like his. Looking back at his own book, Tom opened it directly in the center and was met with hundreds of words sounding like gibberish.

"No, no Tom. Start here," the Captain said calmly flipping the book to the left. In large letters the book read, "Chapter 1: The Beginning". Tom touched the page with his hand and felt it's letters. A fresh scent filled the air and Tom read the first line of his book.

"Thomas Lewis was born," this immediately intrigued Tom. It probably doesn't mean much to you as a reader since we're used to books. But Tom wondered what the book meant by "born". He wondered what the book meant by the word "was".

Tom was hooked. The book was very straightforward in leading into events. He read the first chapter describing himself as a baby who didn't understand anything about the new world around him. He was born to parents who loved him very much and apparently; he was very small. So small his parents could carry him in their arms rocking him back and forth. This made Tom laugh as he read. It was as if his mother was a giant and he was physically being comforted.

The first chapter was odd, but he knew Time was apparently odd in general. He related to this young baby the most because Tom was often confused himself. It reminded Tom of when he sat on the bus and he saw trees, he saw the nighttime, and he saw other people existing. He read about a woman in the hospital who "spanked" his butt. She wore a light blue uniform. The baby didn't understand but her name was Irene. She held him and whispered "Welcome to the world," as she passed him to his mother.

As Tom continued, he read about someone he never met. He read about a Tom living a life in a distant land. But he increasingly related to this character as he continued. The child was even more curious than the baby now that he could use his arms and legs effectively. This new Tom asked questions about life. He wondered why his parents were religious and wondered about other people's beliefs too. He loved science and reading in school. Tom read about this young boy who rode bikes down large hills who scraped his knee. He tried not to cry. Further in the book Tom read about his desire to withhold tears. From his perspective of reading his story, he could see it came from a place of toxic masculinity. The problem seemed very trivial as he now sat reading in the middle of the aisle.

Tom read more about this young boy growing up and going to a place called "high school". It was where Tom met his best friend Eric. His best friend seemed very different in the book than he was in the Community Center. In the book, Eric was a quiet kid. He held his atheism close to his chest because he feared what others thought of him. Tom gravitated toward Eric in the book because he was a curious high school student. Then, Tom turned a page in his book and saw a new chapter. This chapter was called "Experiencing Death".

His mind, of course, spun like it always did. The term "death" was new to Tom. In this chapter he read about his father's death. It was something that struck Tom in the book very hard as he struggled to understand what death meant. As he read the book, Tom saw a clear connection between death and the curtain of the Community Center. He saw how death affected him in the book but also saw how it related to him in the Community Center. Death was something no person would ever return from. But it felt worse because in the Community Center time is non-linear.

Moments on the first floor he never experienced could still come to find him. But in the book when something ended... that was it. Death was the end. Every moment was already experienced, and every second was already spent. Tom in the book began to waver from his happiness into something called depression. The word didn't concern Tom as he was more interested with the events of the book unfolding.

The character of Thomas Lewis was him. He read about Tom meeting a beautiful young woman in a yoga class. Her name was Katherine. He found himself laughing alone as he read about Tom fumbling over his words trying to meet her for the first time. These were the stories Tom was now experiencing for himself through the pages of his own book. Time unfolded one event at a time to equal who he was in the Community Center. He saw the hardships him and Kate had to endure to be together. Before his eyes, he saw exactly the importance of who they were together. A grin split on his face as Tom read about their wedding day. He never experienced their wedding; in the Community Center he was always simply married to Kate.

Life was beautiful for them both. Time moved quickly and Tom worked a well-paying job. Kate started her own yoga business, and they bought a house. And just as everything was at the pinnacle of happiness, the next chapter's title read "The Next Death". Tom was starting to realize the truth about Time. Things continually would get worse with each moment of goodness.

Tom turned the page and read about his mother

passing away. A person he was very close with. His mother was the one who helped him deal with death the first time he experienced it. Tom felt depression filling his soul. His wife tried to be there for him, but Tom was in search of something else. He didn't know what, but he knew it wasn't his wife. He saw Tom in the book begin to question the beliefs he grew up understanding and discovering a part of his mind he never knew he had. He had a deep need to understand what death was and try to find the answers.

Tom continued reading, looking for an answer. Maybe he could find some comfort in knowing this Tom in the book questioned just like he did. He turned the page to the next chapter expecting to see the hope of finding answers. Instead, Tom found hope in another place. Something that made his questions disappear. For the first time in his life and in his existence, Tom did not question anything. He turned the page and read about a baby boy. Tom and Kate had a son.

Chapter XIII

The Story of a Soul

Reading about his son was a beautiful experience. Tom loved his son very much. He wanted him to be anything he wanted. He read about this young boy who was much like himself. Learning to ride a bike or scraping his knee were little similarities he saw in his son that were in his own history.

Funny to use the word history in connection with the Tom of the Community Center. He didn't even understand the word before he ventured to the second floor. But now, he sees the beginning of the book is its history and where he is right now is the present. But, only by his own perspective. Books are continually being read. You only choose when you read them.

Tom's son grew older and around the age of thirteen the chapter ended. Not on a cliff hanger or in a sad way. But Tom quickly flipped through his previous chapter a little confused. Surely, there was more about his son. He didn't even have a name, he only read about short experiences here and there. Tom flipped to the next chapter and decided to keep reading. The next chapter was something Tom wanted to forget he read. Diagnosed with cancer, his wife, died.

Sitting in the middle of the aisle Tom rested the book on his knee looking up for a moment. He didn't understand why his heart was yearning like it did. The death of his wife forced him to stop reading and never want to finish. He tried. But lifting the book and even reading the words of the chapter forced Tom to shake with pain and his arms would lose all strength. They collapsed in his lap holding the book as he stared at the shelves in front of him. His eyes were red realizing Kate would be gone forever.

Tom set the book down. Tears filled his eyes. He was so overwhelmed with existence and the curtain he never considered who he was in the Community Center. What kind of dad was he? What kind of husband was he? What kind of person was he without the loved ones in his life? He wanted to throw the book at the shelf and leave. His wife was dead, and nothing would change the words written in the book. He wanted desperately to try and fix this, but he knew there was no way he could. He wanted to burn the book where it lay and pretend he never came to the second floor, but he knew this would do nothing. Tom wondered if there was any way out of finishing his book.

He stood up in the middle of the aisle holding the book tightly in his hand. He walked down the aisles looking for the Captain. He saw the steps to exit but didn't see him at the top. Quickly, he rushed around different aisles looking for him. Tom turned a corner where the Captain quietly put away books from a small cart. He stood on one of the ladders only a couple feet above Tom's eyeline.

"I don't want to read this," Tom told him forcefully. The Captain grinned and kept putting books away.

"No one ever does," he said as he paused to look at a book in his hand. After a moment of looking at the book the Captain put it onto the shelf thinking about Tom's request. "And for whatever reason you all think that I'm forcing you to finish your books," he said almost smirking. He picked up another book and paused to look at it before putting it back on the shelf.

"What's the point? Why read it? Even if the book is happy, we already know it can't last forever because the book eventually ends!" Tom raised his voice shaking the book in the air. "And if the book is sad, then we're only left alone with our sadness," he concluded lowering the book. Tom tried not to remember what was happening in his book. But his only thoughts remained on his wife. The Captain did not share in Tom's anger and despair. Instead, he let out a small laugh under his breath.

"What's so funny? These are peoples live!" Tom argued with the Captains nonsensical nature.

"It's just that I agree with you, about everything.

Everyone feels the same way you feel about life when they read their pages. I've never met anyone who wasn't at some point very upset by what happened in their lives. I asked the same questions when I read my own book. What's the point? Why not just rip the book up and throw it away?" he continued to laugh and put books up one at a time. "But... in the end... we always keep reading. And eventually, with any luck, we actually finish them," the Captain told Tom as he stopped looking down at him. He could see Tom's defiance to finish the book. "Tell me, what happened in your book so devastating that it destroys the foundation of existence itself?" he sarcastically asked. Tom didn't pick up on the sarcasm as he thought about what the Captain said. He looked down at his book and thought about the life he was leading.

"Kate, my wife, she died. I'm alone with my son. She was taken from me. A good person, taken for no reason," he softly said after a moment. The Captain didn't seem too phased by what he said.

"So, why did she die?" he asked. Tom looked up at the Captain.

"What do you mean why?" Tom asked.

"The book isn't just about you Tom. It *is* you. So, why is your wife dead? Do you hate your wife?" the Captain abruptly asked. Tom was taken back by the accusation.

"No, I don't hate my wife," Tom quickly replied.

"Did you want her to die?" the Captain snapped back as he stared at Tom.

"What? No, I don't want her to die," Tom said growing irritated by the line of questioning.

"It's your book. Maybe she deserved to die," the Captain continued to probe.

"You have no right to talk about Kate like that!" Tom yelled at him.

"Then why did your wife die in *your* book?" the Captain asked again. Tom hoped for some profound message about his motivation to help him continue the book. But the Captain seemed to genuinely want to know why Tom's wife died.

"I can make all these assumptions about you Tom. You can make all these assumptions about yourself. But we will never know why she died until you finish the book," the Captain concluded as he climbed down from the ladder and started to push his carts away.

Tom looked down at his book again. He started to wonder about the things said to him. Something occurred to Tom that wasn't clear before because of his anger. Tom was a father. Tom had a responsibility to his son. Tom needed to be there for someone who didn't understand what was happening. A young boy who only knew his parents love was suddenly alone.

"Can you find my sons book?" Tom asked. The Captain stopped and turned to look at Tom. He was a little confused by the request but knew the book he wanted.

"Follow me," the Captain said motioning for Tom to follow. The two walked down large aisles again only to find a section with very short books. These books were shorter than any others, they maybe only had one or two chapters in them. The Captain went on his knees and pulled a book from the bottom shelf. He placed it in Toms hands. The front cover was a red leather like Tom's book. Embroidered on the front was the name "David Lewis".

Chapter XIV

A Father Meets His Son

"Are you going to be okay?" the Captain asked as Tom stared at the cover of the book in his hands. The name written on the front forced Tom to think heavily on the first events that unfolded when he arrived on the bus. You remember, the first chapter of this book.

"I don't know what to do," Tom replied to the Captain. He didn't expect his son would be named David and didn't expect the book to be so thin.

"Well, you have a story to read. I suggest reading it," the Captain told him nonchalantly.

"What happens when time stands still?" Tom asked almost sarcastically. He was frozen. He didn't know what would happen if time was neither linear nor non-linear.

"Time can't stand still. Each one of these books is

constantly telling a story we choose to read or not. But they are always telling their story," the Captain replied with a hopeful glint in his eye. Tom didn't notice. Slowly, he sat his own book down on the ground. The Captain walked away to leave Tom with his sons book. Tom still didn't notice, only looking at David's book.

He read the cover of the book in front of him again. "David Lewis," he whispered. Tom didn't care about the curtain anymore. He didn't care about why such a cruel thing would happen to his wife. He gave no room in his thoughts to any question burdening him on the first floor. Existence and the Community Center faded away as he stared at the name on the cover of his sons book. Sure, the questions of existence and the curtain would always remain. But Tom gave them no room in his head. He only gave thought to the book in his hands.

He touched the embroidered name on the cover. It's stitching was old as Tom removed dust from it. The book was never used. It was perfect, and he saw no creases along the edges of the spine. The book wasn't heavy. He glanced down at his own book he thought was the weight of the world. But his sons was thin like a magazine. It felt maybe a few chapters in length at most. David Lewis had a short story to tell. Tears filled Tom's eyes as he wondered about the words filling the pages. He wanted David to have a good life. He wanted these pages to be filled with laughter and fun. But he couldn't get over the idea that this David in his hands, was the same David from the bus. He couldn't stop thinking the David on the bus was his son and Tom *did* let this happen. He already saw his wife die that day. He was preparing himself for another sad tale as he flipped open to find out what happened to David. The only way to find out was to open the book and read.

Tom couldn't bring himself to do it. He kept staring at it in his hands. During this moment of frozen time, David's story could be anything Tom wanted it to be. Tom could believe it to be happy instead of sad. It could be hopeful instead of dreadful. David's story didn't have to end, and it could consistently be starting. As long as Tom believed in a story of happiness, then it was the *true* story.

"It isn't true just because you believe it," the Captain said. Tom looked up from the cover. Slowly pushing his cart of books, the Captains eyes were caught by Tom who had still not opened the book. The Captain couldn't force anyone to read the books. He could only keep them and hope one day their stories would have proper breath.

"What do you mean?" Tom asked, his arms were slightly shaking from the tragedy ahead of him. He was only anxious about whatever he'd find in David's book.

"It's nice to think that what we believe is the truth. Or that our belief has any affect on the truth. But we won't ever know until we open the book. We won't ever know until we find out for ourselves," the Captain said. Tom looked down at the book again. The only way to find out was to open it and read. Until then, the truth is only hidden. Not determined by his belief.

"But what does it matter? Why can't I be complacent like everyone else in my belief and thinking it's the right one? Why can't I hold onto a puzzle piece and pretend it fits?" he asked snapping his head back up. The Captain thought for a moment. It was a good question after all. It's the one most people in the Community Center agree on. These things don't matter to them because your belief is the only thing that matters. You have to keep your head down and believe without certainty. This will earn you the right to a peaceful existence.

"This isn't about some metaphor like a puzzle missing a piece Tom. If you only ever pretend your puzzle piece matters then you'll never finish your own story. After all, we are souls. Your soul is only the thing reading the story of your life. That's what we are. And if you don't read it, then you will never know," he said as he pointed to the book next to Tom on the ground. Tom looked down and saw his own book laying there. He stopped reading his story the moment he found out about Kates death. And now he looked at his sons book unsure if he'd be able to read it either.

The Captain put his hands back on the cart and walked away. Tom stared at the empty space where he was. He leaned his back against the shelves. Looking down at David's book, he took a deep breath. His hand opened it slightly with only his index finger. Like ripping off a band-aid, Tom quickly opened it to the first page. In the center of that old manila page were the words "Chapter One: Alone". Tom quickly shut the book again. He knew it. It's a sad story. It was a sad book and the Captain wanted him to read it so he could finish his own book.

But why? Why was Tom supposed to read either of these? Why was Tom supposed to subject himself to understanding Time and the curtain in such terrible means? Why did it hurt so much to understand who he was as a person? These questions were flooding his head like many others often did. He looked down at the book and read David's name again. It wasn't his own. It wasn't about Tom right now. It wasn't about whether he understood things or not. It was about his sons voice being heard in the sea of books he stood in. Each one of them unique and different but all encompassed by this thing called Time. Each books moments happening concurrently until someone picks it up and reads its linear tale. This was David's book. This was the book that would be heard today in the tidal wave of stories. Tom opened the book again making sure his sons voice would be heard. David's first chapter was "Alone" and so that's what Tom would hear.

He flipped past the first title page. He read about his son's birth. It felt normal. It felt much like his own birth. It was different reading this birth from the perspective of his son. David was born like most people, confused and curious. He didn't know where he was or why he was. He didn't have a concept of space or taking up space. Tom read about David seeing Kate for the first time. He cried very loudly but instinctively knew she was his mother. He held her tight and she returned his comfort. He loved being held and loved by her.

David didn't remember Tom being there. And Tom began to see the absent father he really was. For the entirety of the chapter he read about his son; but in his own book, he believed he was always there for his son. Thirteen years of his sons life were condensed to a single chapter in Tom's book. He was never truly there for his son. He could see the toll Tom's absence took in David's book. The shadows of stress and anxiety were long and lingering over David's life as Kate did her best to comfort him. He would hear his mother crying in the bed alone when Tom was out on a business trip. As David grew older he was much angrier than Tom remembered from his own book. The contrast was unbearable to see as it played out in front of his eyes.

Kate was diagnosed with cancer. And from David's perspective, Tom's meeting at work was equivalent to ignoring his mother. This left David often sitting with his mother at the hospital. He would look at her face slowly fade away into nothingness. David watered a festering hatred for his father and soon, depression clawed into his mind. Tom's eyes slowly read the pages as he saw his son already facing these shadows alone. He wiped a tear away from his face and read on.

David grew very close to his mother until there was nothing left to draw close to. Tom received a call from the hospital. But David was there when it happened. Time moved quickly for David after it happened and yet nothing was happening in his book. Days bled together as Tom read the pages of David's book. The depression and anger leaping from the pages of David's book made it increasingly difficult to continue. As he read, Tom began to hate himself for ignoring the needs of his son. But his wife died, and now all that was left were the questions of the universe. These assumptions people had built in their mind eventually lead to a psychological structure on a shaky foundation at best.

One afternoon Tom found his son drunk from a bottle of liquor. Of course, Tom was furious with his thirteen year old son. He yelled and screamed but nothing was getting through to the young boy. There was too much of a wound and too much hurt. Tom's incessant questioning turned on his own son asking him "What is wrong with you?"

David went quiet as his body wavered back and forth from the alcohol. All he said was "I want to go back... it was safe then... I just want to go back." And what did Tom do? Did he rush and hug his son who desperately needed him? Did he understand and try to comfort his son who clearly missed Kate probably more than he did? No, Tom only sighed. Tom sighed and it was the catalyst that pushed David to jump from the bridge later that evening. Tom turned the page... but there were no more pages.

Chapter XV

The State of Being

"Your son is dead, Tom," the Captain said sitting next to him. Tom stared at the last page of David's book. This book Tom held was not as particularly nice as he'd wishfully hoped. Its pages were filled with mistakes and Tom's own unwillingness to take responsibility for those mistakes. Maybe it was a perception that they were his mistakes in the first place.

But Tom didn't much care for any of those dire questions any longer. Yes, they existed beneath the surface of the deep, but Tom only sat staring at the pages, knowing his son was gone forever. Only the memories of his son could fill the chapters of other books. Only his being could linger through other people's stories. The Captain did not try to comfort Tom. He did not try to dis-sway Tom from experiencing any emotion that may have come into Tom's body. But rather, he told Tom to embrace the truth by showing it to him.

"Your son, David, is dead," the Captain repeated. He saw a tear run down Tom's cheek. Tom let it fall and hit the page beneath him. It soaked into the book and became a part of its own structure. The books construction was a part of Tom and Tom a part of it. These pages expressed a world he would never feel more connected with. But now, more than ever, wanted to separate entirely.

"I was told I would see why David went behind the curtain on the second floor," Tom whispered under his breath. The Captain could sense that Tom felt lied to and betrayed. This wasn't uncommon in the realm of Time. Often, people see the mistakes of themselves more prominently when time is linear. Put into this context, people see the perceived natural evil of humanity and its obvious hubris.

"Without these books, Tom, we only get a glimpse at what we are on the first floor," the Captain quietly replied.

"And what are we!" Tom suddenly jolted with electric energy slamming the book shut. He stared at the Captain who was unmoved by the sudden outburst. He only stared at the ground feeling like a child who pulled at grass simply because it was there.

"I told you Tom, we are the souls reading the stories of our lives," the Captain said. This analogy was true in the sense that anything anyone says can be true.

"Who wrote these books? Everything in existence

was built by someone on the first floor. This entire building was constructed by us. Even the second floor is the construction of people in existence. So who wrote these books?" Tom asked with intensity, apathetic to the Captains analogies. He quickly stood up still holding the book in his hand. "Someone here must have written these. Is that what's beyond the curtain? Some otherworldly being who authored these books. Maybe that's the key to understanding existence. Maybe there's a connection between some heavenly god and these books," Tom said frantically. The Captain quietly sat listening to Tom's ranting as he continually collected theories.

"Tom, you're not going to find the answer to what's after the curtain. Not by philosophies sake or by continually questioning," The Captain said calmly.

"Then you tell me, tell me who wrote these books," Tom asked a third time. The Captain stood up and walked back to his cart.

"We all write our own books," he said as he pushed the small cart. But this ham-fisted reply wasn't good enough for Tom.

"If we write our own books then that's an answer. So we do have at least one answer!" Tom told him following close behind. The Captain was growing irritable and bored of the rabbit hole that he believed never ended.

"What do you mean?" he reluctantly replied.

"I mean if we write our own books then God didn't create us. We create ourselves. Which means we are god," Tom said feeling superior in his answer. He felt his skin itch as he wanted to keep digging where there were no more places to go. The Captain stopped walking and turned to Tom. His face was dire and radiated a sense of urgency. He lifted his finger as if to start to berate Tom but lowered it after giving some thought to his actions. The Captain knew arguing with Tom would only push him to keep digging. Instead of following where the winding labyrinth eventually lead, the Captain gave a concrete solution.

"You're not stupid Tom. There are things in the Community Center not created by men nor created by natural events," he said turning back to the cart and beginning to push again.

"I've got nothing but a dead son and questions that have no answers! Stop talking to me like every conversation has to be a test for me to figure out!" Tom yelled at the Captain who abruptly did not think on his actions any longer. He only had action to give.

"You lost your son Tom! Think! Think for a moment! Stop asking questions for one second and embrace the ripping apart of your heart!" the Captain yelled at him. Tom stepped back stunned by the sudden outburst.

Looking down at the book Tom still held in his hand, he could see the Captains view. It was true. Finding out about his sons' death only pushed Tom to try and find more answers no matter where he found them. Tom even considered himself and everyone else to be gods. But creating life wasn't what made anyone a god. Creating life was only another ability on a long scale of what beings could and could not do within existence. Even if everything in the Community Center was created and built by some other worldly being, that "being" still fell on the scale of what anyone in existence could or could not do. And as long as there is a scale, then whatever beings possess it will never know if they are the top or the bottom.

This forced Tom to think about his own heart and where he fell on the scale of existence. Equally, it's what most people experience every day in their own books. Walking through life they wonder where they fall on this scale of power, beauty, importance etc. People like to think that because they fall somewhere higher on any particular scale that they hold any more importance than anyone else. If someone is sad then people compare and think if they've ever experienced sadness as intense. When you are sad, you wonder if you are a burden on others because your sadness isn't the worst a person has experienced on the scale of existence. But, for a few moments in these books there is a purity in human experiences. There are no comparisons, there is no scale, and there is no burden. There is only... *something.*

And so, Tom's heart ached. He grabbed his chest and felt its strings convulse with absolute pain. The Captain blurred from view. Tom only saw the haze of tears filling his eyes as he fell to his knees. There was no room to question. He didn't think about what he could have done to save David. He didn't think about Kate or religion. The monotony of the ballot disappeared from his mind as his chest pounded. His mind was an enigma of being absolute emptiness yet never being so full. Tom experienced for the first time whatever it was he needed to feel and experience. The agony of losing his son pulsed within him. He wept on the floor of the second floor. David's book dropped to the ground and Tom's vulnerability radiated from himself.

I can't stress the importance of these moments for Tom or you. Yes, even you dear reader. Whoever you are with your social groups, family, and friends. At what moments in life do you remember only *being*? The intensity of being absolutely sad where you are no longer *feeling* sad, but you *are* sadness. If you are incredibly lucky maybe it was a time when you experienced absolute happiness. A moment where you don't think about anything else but the moment of being in joy. You don't think about sharing in your joy because nothing else exists except that joy. Time stands still as you stare at the words in your book never wanting to read forward because you know the moment will end. Of course, I'm not saying sharing these moments isn't important or finishing the book isn't important. But there is nothing else if not the moment you're currently reading in your book. There is nothing else except for the current chapter, the current page, or the current word you are reading right now. Every chapter, every page, every current word is constantly being read.

Tom discovered this in a disheartening way. He discovered this through the death of his son and understood what it meant to truly just *be*. But it wasn't so far gone before he once again noticed his own book on the ground. Before he noticed his tears begin to fade, and the questions of existence creeping back into his mind, Tom noticed his unfinished book.

"The moment is still here," the Captain said watching Tom come back to normality. Tom breathed heavily still on his knees and looking at his book. "Every moment is exactly as the one you just experienced, but we only let outside events take it away from us," the Captain continued.

And if this were a book about living in the moment and not concerning yourself with the past or future then I would be inclined to agree with the Captain. If this were a book about existence's unknowing chaos and to ignore those distractions so you might eventually find peace, then I would agree with the Captain. But this book isn't about that and neither is all of existence. Embracing the happiness and pain of life instead of worrying about its past or future is yet another answer people have found to believe in. Living in the moment is to ignore every moment, past or future. Yet, this is not a belief. It's simply a part of life one can choose to experience or not. Tom knew this as he heard the Captain say every moment should be like the one he just experienced. He didn't argue with him because he saw now that the Captain had an answer for existence just like everyone else on the first floor. The Captain only chose to live in the moment instead of worrying about what the future or past may hold.

Tom enjoyed this belief. Tom experienced this

belief firsthand as he would always carry the burden of losing his own son with him. Through this moment Tom understood something else sitting on his knees in front of the Captain. He grinned slightly with dried tears still across his face.

"What is it?" the Captain asked. Tom understood that no matter what belief someone held, they were right. It didn't matter if they believed in living in the moment, or an omnipotent being who created everything. Whatever belief they held, that person was right. From an old atheist friend to a professor seeking evil, and the keeper of books only wanting to live in the moment. They all believed they were right and so, they were all *right*.

Tom didn't care for being *right*. He didn't care about his own biases with Christianity. If he went beyond the curtain and was sent to hell for eternity, he would still question. If he went beyond the curtain and he was met by a giant chicken he would *definitely* question. This specific one made Tom laugh. The ridiculousness of going behind the curtain and there's a literal large chicken just staring at him. No answers. The chicken can't speak. It's just there looking at you. You and a giant chicken for the rest of eternity. And yet, this strange belief is just as ridiculous and valid as any other belief on the ballot. So, Tom smiled.

"It's nothing," Tom said taking a moment. He stood up from his place and picked up his own book. "Thank you," he told the old Captain now seeing him in a different light. He no longer saw the Captain as the keeper of great truths in a fantastical land known as Time. He saw the Captain as just another person with another answer in existence.

"Of course, Tom. Enjoy the rest of your book. I'm curious to see what you find," the Captain said as he pushed his cart away. Tom looked down at his book again. He walked back to where he sat. As he did he saw the stairs in the distance leading out of from the second floor. Looking around, Tom decided to leave the second floor and seek more through its pages on the first. Tom stole his own book.

Chapter XVI

God and Church

In the following pages our protagonist Tom found himself sitting in a church during a normal sermon. He didn't know if this church was one his parents attended or if it was a popular church amongst the Christian believers. He didn't think to ask what denomination it fell into or if the church supported differing beliefs outside the normal understanding of Christianity. He simply sat next to a woman who looked possibly a little younger than his mother. She wore a nice conservative Sunday dress. She looked polite with a dash of sternness in her eyes. On the other side of the woman were a few other people he couldn't see very well. To Tom's right was a man with a nice plaid shirt, bright blue jeans, and noticeably short hair. His forehead was sharp and looked constricted. This made Tom think the man was much sterner than the woman. He was a well-built man who looked as though he worked in construction most his life. The reflections of what these people were in their own books was ever prevalent.

This reminded Tom of his own book stuffed underneath his shirt. And you're probably wondering yourself how Tom went from leaving the second floor to the middle of a large congregation on a Sunday morning. Tom didn't wonder how he ended up here. He was happy to be back on the first floor and understood time was moving differently. Although, he still held onto his own book hidden underneath his shirt.

"It's the choices we make that define us!" the preacher yelled in front of the congregation.

"Are they?" Tom (of course) thought to himself.

Now, the preacher was a man of strict conviction who spoke clearly with authority. He was someone who didn't waver in his faith attempting his best efforts to transfer his faith onto his congregation. Characteristically, Tom started to wonder. Who gave the preacher authority to speak on such matters of life's choices? Who gave the preacher the leadership to speak on God and man? Was it his own existence giving itself authority over other existences? But, what gave Tom the authority to question the fellow consciousness? Tom wondered if the congregation only collected weekly to comfort themselves from the terrible fact that none of them knew what was behind the curtain. The preacher was brave and stoic, but he spoke a sermon that felt sincere and real compared to what Tom already knew.

The sermon wasn't about the curtain or an eternal damnation, but it followed more how one should live one's life according to the Bibles will. But we're not here to only talk about Tom's current thoughts. Lord (no pun intended) knows we've done that enough. So, something distracted Tom's thoughts along with a few others in the congregation.

A muffled voice was heard near a stained-glass window portraying the story of Noah. The muffled voice was not quiet and sounded extremely angry. A shadow fell over the window opposite to a large concrete area surrounding the church. The shadow was a silhouette of a person raising their hand high above them and shaking it violently. Suddenly another shadow fell on the glass. This time it was of another person holding a large sign. It took a few moments for Tom to understand the muffled voice, but it suddenly was clear for him and many others seated quietly.

"Racist bigots!" he heard the voice vibrate against the glass. Tom wondered if the voices were referring to the entirety of Christianity or this specific church. Possibly the people yelled about an individual in the church or maybe the entire congregation.

The woman sitting next to Tom looked noticeably agitated even more than the rest of the congregation. Her eyes winced as they would occasionally glance at the windows. Rightfully so, she feared for her safety in the congregation. The people outside reminded Tom much of the men and women in the place called "politics" his mother gave title to.

The woman sighed and looked back to the front of the church. This was a loud sigh several people overheard. A few looked at her with agreement. Tom didn't disagree. The muffled sound of anger outside the building forced him to think about what he might find when he walks outside. Out of all his experiences he'd never been met with violent outbursts by anyone.

"It'll be okay, Ma'am," the man on the right side of Tom said. The man had a slight grin on his face, but his eyes still squinted with sternness as if he were staring directly into the sun. His voice was slow and long winded with an accent sounding almost like another language. But this didn't take away from the warmth in his voice. It was comforting to hear. Tom couldn't tell if the sudden comfort was from the man clearly being much stronger than anyone else or if it was simply the voice of the man which brought a particularly warm strength.

"How can you say it will be okay?" the woman snapped at the man with a restrained whisper. A few faces slightly turned to hear the conversation transpiring as the preacher continued to speak. Tom awkwardly widened his eyes as some of them looked in his direction; knowing he was not involved in the conversation but listening on with the rest of them.

"They're degenerates interrupting the churches service. We've done nothing wrong. Why bother us?" the woman continued hurriedly like she had somewhere to be other than sitting in the middle of the pews. The man didn't say anything at all. He glanced down at the wooden pew in front of him for a moment, giving thought to what she said. After a moment of thought, the man raised his head to continue looking forward. Tom noticed there were no other people past where the man sat. Every pew in the church was filled with different people. But just past the man there were missing only a few seats. It was almost odd to see.

The preacher concluded his sermon in prayer everyone joined in on. Tom did as well with respect to everyone else but was unaware if he were truly speaking to God or not. The congregation then slowly started to stand and greet each other in fellowship. Some people immediately left, and some others stood around mingling with one another. As Tom stood to exit the pew he saw the woman start to walk away only stopped by the man who sat to the right of Tom.

"We *have* done wrong, Ma'am," he told her. He referred to the Christian (and religious) idea that every person has done wrong in some form. Every person was full of sin in need of redemption.

"Oh posh, I obviously didn't mean in the sense that we aren't all sinners. Of course we are!" she said almost gleefully but radiating with sarcasm. "I only mean we haven't done any direct wrong to those people outside with their signs and provocative actions," she said pointing a stern finger to the window still containing the shadow of angry protestors. "And so they should not be so riled about what goes on in here. This place. A place of worship to God," she concluded speaking. The man stood in front of her still with squinted eyes and contemplating what he would say.

"A place of worship to God ma'am?" he finally said repeating her words with a grin. This clearly heated her even further as it seemed the man was mocking her.

"Yes. This place of worship," she said. Her leg slightly moved, and Tom thought the poor women would actually slam her foot down like a child.

"Ma'am, you're in here and they're out there. The only difference between you is the space between," the man told her.

Tom thought on this. What was the difference between the angry protestors outside and the people inside? Surely there were more differences than the simplicity of space. Tom thought the difference between them would obviously be that of religious and non-religious. The beliefs people held had to be the crux which separated people. At it's core you have a group outside who did not believe in God, and the group inside who do believe in God. But it weren't always true. Looking at the entire Community Center, Tom knew the greatest separation between people weren't their beliefs. Phestiles and Acedia both had citizens of the same belief. What was it separating those inside the church and those outside?

The woman was not pleased with the man's answer. She saw it almost as a personal insult to her character rather than a path of understanding the man offered. Instead of taking the path, the woman abruptly turned and walked away, this time clomping her feet down with every step. Tom and the man watched her leave as Tom walked closer to him. The man continued watching the woman then glanced to the stain-glass window watching the anger unfold outside.

"I don't understand. How is the only difference between you and them the space between?" Tom asked innocently. The man looked at Tom. There was a simplicity about Tom the man enjoyed. Although the man spoke with deep words, it was as if those words came naturally to him without much need for diving into questions. The man looked around the church they stood in. It was a beautiful church with large wooden pillars and red carpet you could probably sleep on. Its air was filled with fellowship and color spilling in from the stained windows.

"Those out there, with their signs and anger; they don't believe in God," the man said continuing to look at the church. "And they see everything we do in here as an attack on their basic livelihood. If we disagree with how they live then we have attacked them. Also it's because they don't believe in god," he continued still trying to think of what exactly he wanted to convey. But Tom could see it wasn't as if the man were making things up as he went. The man considered Tom's question critically. With every word the man spoke Tom thought someone whispered the answer in his ear.

"And us in here, we believe in God. But that doesn't make us much different," his eyes then paused on something. Tom looked where he stared and saw the woman from before. "The woman I just spoke with is angry. She's spiteful I would suggest she could ever be similar to someone out there," he said as they both watched her. She was now chatting with other people and occasionally glanced at Tom and the man. The group she was talking with occasionally would glance with her as if she were angrily talking about what the man said.

"If a Satanic church opened across from this Christian church she would be the first in line to hold a sign of anger at them. She would claim the Satanist church was only there to attack her basic livelihood because she disagrees with how they live," he continued. Tom could see the similarities the man pointed out. He was painting a picture that the anger of the woman and the anger of the protestors were ultimately two sides of the same coin. Two types of people with different beliefs brought together by anger.

"So then how do we fix societies problems? If we don't understand each belief and try to figure out which one is actually beneficial and which ones aren't?" Tom asked the man. He thought again for a moment carefully considering what to say. Tom thought the man would take a nihilistic approach. There's no point to anything and so there's no point in even trying to be better.

"You agree some beliefs are beneficial, and some are not?" he asked Tom who was warming up to the man's long drawn-out accent. Tom nodded in an obvious manner. It was something he thought everyone agreed on at least. Some beliefs were clearly better for society and others weren't.

"Is Christianity the most beneficial belief?" the man asked. Tom didn't answer the question. Christianity is something he followed his entire life. But learning more about himself in his own book, he wondered the reasons why he followed Christianity in the first place. Did he only not want to feel the guilt from David's death? Did he follow only because he was told to follow? And in that sense, Tom didn't think Christianity was beneficial. But who was he to decide?

"What is beneficial?" Tom asked softly after a moment.

"Yup," the man said, his accent beginning high and dipping into a low-voiced agreement. "But also, how do you know to ask, 'what is beneficial'? The curtain? Do you look at the curtain and think to yourself 'there is no way to know anything if we don't know what's after the curtain?'," the man asked looking back at Tom. "And what of those protesting outside?" he asked giving a small point to the windows and looking at their silhouettes. "What discredits what they believe as beneficial or not? Fear for what's after the curtain? The woman I spoke with earlier is now complaining about what I said to the preacher," he moved his finger towards the woman. Sure enough, Tom saw the woman speaking with the preacher about what the man said. The preacher looked almost squirmy and nervous as he occasionally glanced at the man.

"Will the preacher think it's beneficial to ban me from the church? Or will he think it's beneficial to let me continue to worship here? And where does he understand his answers? Is it based on what the woman wants or what *he* wants? What is beneficial and who decides?" the man kept asking question after question as he snowballed. Tom's head was spinning and couldn't believe he met someone who was asking as many questions he normally did. But it was also someone who clearly believed in God. Someone who had a strong conviction to a particular faith but still questioned in ways not always appropriate to his own religion.

"What do you believe?" Tom asked abruptly but the man wasn't caught off guard. The man was a brick wall against any question Tom could ask. Not because he had the answers, but maybe because the man was a part of the questions also.

"There is God. There is nothing else. He is love and He is good. Darkness and evil is only the absence of Him. Darkness is when *I* say what is beneficial and not what *He* says is beneficial," the man explained. It was the first time Tom felt real meaning behind the words Christianity. Instead of words people spoke in passing or the words plainly printed on the ballot.

"What about other beliefs though? Hinduism? Islam?" Tom asked curiously.

"What about them?" the man asked genuinely curious by what Tom meant.

"If your belief is right then doesn't that mean multitudes of people are wrong? Those people get sent to eternal damnation? Hell?" Tom asked not believing the words he said as he said them. He had a difficult time comprehending eternal damnation and the idea even if someone *chose* hell, they eventually wouldn't want to *leave* hell.

"It is not for me to call any person unclean. I revert you to what I said is beneficial or not. Do I tell someone they are going to hell because I believe it is beneficial for them to believe what I believe? Or do I sacrifice my own wants and ask what God wants? Will people go to hell? It is not my place. Will people go to heaven? It is not my place," the man said sternly and with absolute conviction. It sounded good but also sounded as if the man were only a slave to his God.

"What if you're sent to hell?"

"Then I am sent to hell by His will," he said. Tom almost scoffed. How could any person answer that question truthfully?

"And what if you lose everything? What if you lose all you have, everyone you love, and all you have is the curtain staring at you as it begs for you to give up and walk through it?" Tom asked almost becoming angry like the protestors outside.

"Then it is His will," the man said holding his ground. Tom was annoyed by this answer.

"How could you ever know how you'd react to such loss?" Tom asked frustratingly.

"Because it happened," the man concluded lowering his head. His eyes looked to the ground now and Tom's breath fell short. Tom looked back at the pew where they sat during the sermon. He saw the empty spaces where the man originally sat. He looked back at the man. A small tear rolled down his cheek, but Tom could see it wasn't the man giving up. He was feeling. His heart hurt. The man felt the weight of absolute nothingness press against his soul. He felt this moment.

Tom was frozen. He didn't know how to respond to the man's predicament. This man was at the point in his book where everything was gone, and yet the man continued to follow his God. Tom felt his book pressed against his shirt. He wondered if he would eventually truly find God and follow him as willingly as this man. Tom put his hand on the man's back attempting to give any sort of comfort. It was a nice gesture to attempt but the man was strong in his convictions. He was at peace no matter how much he was given room to cry. Tom felt the pressure even further to finish his own book.

Chapter XVII

The Guilty Pay

Tom felt the elevator descend to the first floor. He thought about what he would do with his book and how he felt unable to finish it. He lifted the book in front of him and read his name written brightly across the front. Would he ever be able to finish it? Would he ever want to finish it? Was it normal that Tom didn't want to finish it? If I could answer Tom then I would say sure, most people don't want to finish their stories. No one wants to face death and the conclusion of life. Whether finishing their life means losing all they love in existence or because finishing life means the fear of what's beyond the curtain.

Was Tom going to get in trouble for taking his book to the first floor? He did not know. But how could he be in trouble at all? The only thing they could threaten him with was finishing his book. Anything else was on this side of the curtain. What was beneficial? He thought about what he was told by the man in the church. How Tom should follow what the man's God wanted and not what Tom wanted. But that's the whole crux of every book isn't it? Who is right? Who is wrong? Who is good and who is evil? The question the man proposed was there was no good versus evil but only what *you* want versus what *God* wants.

And clearly by most of Tom's book he'd not followed this philosophy of doing what God wants. His book was about a terrible man who did awful things to his family. He was a man who did not deserve to have his book finished. It was a story about a pain weighing on the soul you've been reading about. This pain so recognizable to most of us it seems almost fleeting and useless at times. It was the feeling of guilt growing inside of him like a seed giving forth nothing but dangerous vines covered in thorns. They tore at Tom's soul as they wrapped around his existence. He only ever understood a path to give up and give in. This apathy for guilt did not negate his desire to be a better man to his wife and his son. But he knew he only watered the seed of guilt for it to grow stronger against him. A never-ending field overgrown with guilt and despair took his life as he stood in the elevator staring at what he believed to be a godforsaken book. There was nothing he could do about it. The book does not change. No one's book changes once it is written in the pages. It is written and it is done.

What does a person do when faced with an excruciating and inescapable guilt? What can a person do? What can a person do against a deserved guilt? Anything they do will only be seen as a way to weasel out of punishment to save their own skin.

The elevator slowed to a stop while Tom stared at his book thinking about these topics and even thinking how his own thought process sounded as a way to wiggle his way out of deserved punishment; only adding to the guilt. The doors slid open and where Tom expected to find Clive waiting for him, he was taken back by someone with a slim familiarity. It was a woman. The vague memory of her floated around his mind with Tom unable to remember who she was. Stress radiated from her being as her body slightly shook. Dark stains clouded her eyes with various wrinkles covering her face in age. Strings of hair lay on her shoulders following up to the tips of her head. Tom (for a brief moment) felt incredibly unsettled. Thankfully, the woman obliged him and was able to cure Tom of his discomfort rather quickly. The woman swung a large block of wood at Tom impacting his forehead and knocking him unconscious. He fell to the floor feeling as though his skull rattled around like a can of spray paint. Face down and his book loose in his hand the woman took it from him. For a brief moment he felt his body dragging across the floor outside the elevator until he passed out completely.

Now, in the next moments the recesses of Tom's mind were not empty. Although the dreams Tom had would not be remembered. His dream sat him in the body of his book. Tom sat in his car; he stared at his phone before going up to his apartment. His cell phone had various texts from family members who were attempting to reach out and make sure he was okay as he'd just lost his son and previously his wife. Tom put his phone down not wanting to read the comforting texts. He wore a suit jacket with several stains covering it. His hair hadn't been washed in weeks and his eyes were red from the unstoppable crying and stress. He reached to his passenger seat and picked up a book called "Bible". You've probably heard of it. It's a popular one. Tom got out of his car and closed the door looking up at his apartment giving a sigh. And although Tom wouldn't remember the current dream, he felt a connection with who this Tom was.

"I just want to know who you are. I want to know you are real. I want to know what happens after we die. Where are they?" Tom asked under his breath looking up towards a grey sky and lightly falling snow.

He opened the door to his apartment where darkness covered every inch. He walked inside and set his things down. He walked to the refrigerator where he found the ingredients to make a sandwich his son insisted was the best type of sandwich. He closed the door and grabbed the bottle of liquor on top of the fridge his son never finished. He took a swig, and just like David had to hold himself from spitting it out, so did he. Tom was never much of a drinker. But his guilt kept him going as he walked back to the living room sitting on the couch alone. Suddenly there was a knock at his door. Tom stood up and slowly walked to the door. Opening, he saw a woman frantic and angry standing at his threshold.

Tom slowly opened his eyes from the dream. Fragments remained but quickly disappeared into the darkness of his mind. A blurry scene now surrounded him. He could feel sharp blades of grass sliding across his face. The comfort of cool night air brushed against his cheek and the blue sheen of nighttime bled through the glass dome far above him. He noticed it was not the grass sliding against his face but his face dragging across the grass. He looked down and saw someone holding his foot, dragging him to the only place he knew in the Community Center to have a large dome looking into the clouds above. In shock, Tom pulled his foot from her. She willingly dropped it and stood staring at the large black curtain she brought him to. Tom had never been this close to it. It towered over them looking much taller than before. The woman didn't look at its size, she only stared at its fabric holding a book at her side. She was calm, no longer shaking with stress and presumably anger, but a stillness Tom felt uncomfortable.

Tom held his head and tried to stand stumbling slightly. He tapped his forehead where he could feel his injury. A dark liquid dot transferred from his wound to his finger. It looked black in the darkness of the park, but he couldn't tell if it were just because it were dark or if it had a different color. He tried to collect his thoughts at the situation he found himself in. His eyes widened as he realized the woman held his book at her side.

"You want it back don't you," she asked calmly. Her voice sounding elderly for someone who did not look too elderly. "Why? If you haven't finished it yet why would you finish it now?" she asked him almost sickened by his inability to read it's pages. "Oh yes, I know you haven't finished it. Why else steal it?" she asked turning and looking at him. Her crazed eyes were not soft but plagued by pain. Her physical appearance hadn't changed but she didn't look as though she was going to hit him again with the plank.

"What? Who are you?" Tom asked grasping his head a little disoriented. He glanced around at the park. He'd never seen it at night and saw dim lights lining it's circular walls. People still watching the curtain as friends and family entered through it. Loud cries were heard echoing in the large biome mixed with bouts of laughter and murmured whispers. No one gave much glance to the two of them standing so close to the curtain.

"I read your book. You know who I am," she said softly again as if Tom did know who she was. To an extent Tom did recognize her.

"Why did you read my book?" he asked after a moment of silence.

"It's all about you isn't it?" she asked, her anger slowly raising in her voice. "You can't even stand to remain on a question that revolves around anything else but yourself!" she said shaking the book. The woman's voice was now much louder, and Tom did not remember her face as much, but the voice of her yelling broke through to him. She had a crazed look about her, a shrieking voice, a woman who'd yelled at him before. This was the woman who yelled at him the moment he saw David walk through the curtain. The woman who knew it was Tom's fault. He could hide from anyone but this woman. She was the embodiment of his own guilt standing in front of him.

"Ms. Bryant... Lindsey Bryant," Tom said suddenly with a lowered voice. She would not admit it but she was slightly taken back by him actually remembering her. They'd only met a handful of times but according to Tom's own book was supposed to meet several more times. "You were my sons' teacher. A caring soul who tried her best to keep my son on a good path," Tom said.

"He wanted so much for you to love him but all he could do was hate you," she said walking closer to Tom and placing her hand on his back. "He hated you though. Your son hated you with everything within himself," she whispered in Tom's ear wanting him to feel her pain. Suddenly, he felt himself pushed to the ground in front of the curtain. The fabric of its weight not an inch from his nose. Fear consumed Tom and he pushed himself away from its flowing cloak. Turning around he could see she quickly switched to her more violent self. Someone who would easily push him through.

"This is it," Tom thought to himself. The line between life and death was blurring. This had to be where his book ended. This is where he would see what was behind the curtain and who was finally *right* in the end. This woman who tried to help David was devastated by his suicide to the point where she felt Tom's own existence should be paid for it. But even she did not know what was behind the curtain. She was only the mirror of his own guilt and sin.

"He HATED you!" she violently screamed at him arching her back as to force herself to scream louder. She did not lie. But not telling a lie isn't the same as telling the truth. Tom was particularly good at discerning what a lie was and things that weren't lies. But very few can look and determine what is truth in the end. Tom knew he was a bad person, and this was not a lie. Tom knew what she wanted to do to him and that he deserved it. This was also... not a lie. But was it beneficial to her? Or to the world? Or was it beneficial to a David now far beyond the curtain? Maybe it was beneficial to the God the man spoke about in the church and his will? How would Tom ever know the difference between the two?

"This is your fault. This is all your fault," she said pacing back and forth. "It can't be. This can't be the way. How is this the way! It's not me! That's not me!" she stopped pacing and yelled towards the glass dome above them. Her anger slowly turned into a sadness escaping her eyes. Sniffling, she walked close to Tom with her head hung low. Suddenly he felt her hands grab his shirt and pulled him close to her. Toms foot moved back and felt the curtains fabric on his shoe. Every path of what could be behind the curtain flashed through his mind. Burning eternally in hell for the terrible things he'd done felt as real as a simple step. Pain the likes of which he would never comprehend and how his fear only strengthened his deserving of that pain. It was only a step away. Tom knew deep down that it's what he deserved no matter what happened. The woman had his life in his hands. The woman's anger amplified his own guilt and there was nothing but darkness between the two of them. Her eyes seared into his. Tears filled them and ran down her face as she looked at Tom's field of guilt tearing apart his soul. She wanted badly for Tom to suffer in his thorns. All she saw were dead eyes and the pain of a teenager who never knew his father.

Her embrace was something neither of them expected nor understood. Her face fell on his chest and Tom couldn't move by her arms wrapped around him. He didn't understand, but neither did she. From absolutely no belief on the ballot did Tom deserve anything other than to be thrown behind the curtain. Was this hug beneficial to her? Was she only hugging him so she wouldn't later feel the guilt of throwing him through the curtain? Was this what the man's God wanted? Tom did not know. But Tom learned a different type of breaking in this moment. It was a brokenness different from when he felt broken by the weight of guilt. Tom broke in tears and embraced her because he simply needed someone to hug. The thorns of those vines were not gone but hugging this woman felt as though there was something to understand on this side of the curtain. The two held each other knowing there was no reason for either of them to care. In darkness of hatred and anger, the impossible happened, light was formed.

Chapter XVIII

A Sandwich and Liquor

David placed the two slices of bread next to each other on a paper plate. He took the plate and set it on the fake marble counter of the small two-bedroom apartment. David opened the refrigerator and took out a package of honey ham. He took off the lid and a slight scent of an unpleasant stench entered his nostrils. He made a face at the smell and assumed the ham had gone bad. Doing his best to ignore the stench, David took out three slices and folded them placing them on one slice of the white bread. He took the container of ham and placed it back in the fridge exactly how it sat before with no error.

Returning things the way they were was particularly important to David. The significance of this came down to the apartment being exactly in the same place it'd been when his mother passed away not too long ago. The ham was facing outwards towards the opening of the door with the entirety of the space it took on the left of the shelf. David even nudged the container slightly positioning it in what he believed was exactly where his mother left it.

He then looked to the fridge door where a bottle of mustard lay flat on its side. No doubt it had fallen when his mother used it last and closed the door. Regardless, it was where it would be placed back as well. David shook the bottle and heard the sloshing of goop inside of it. He opened the cap and dotted the ham with two eyes and a small curve underneath forming a smile. He quickly turned his head from it and walked back to the refrigerator. He lay the mustard on its side, exactly where it was supposed to be. Shutting the fridge door he then reached above it to find a bag of potato chips sitting next to a bottle of liquor. This bottle was his mother's also. She was the one who enjoyed a glass every so often, his father never drank to his knowledge. The chips were half empty, and David took out a handful placing them on top of the mustard smiling face. His stomach sank as he glimpsed at the smile for only a moment. He hid his sinking feeling beneath the actions he quickly took ignoring the emotions growing inside. He placed the chips back on top of the fridge and looked at the full bottle of liquor. He'd tasted alcohol only once. It had a stinging bitterness to him but knew it helped his mother unwind. He walked back to his sandwich and placed the empty slice of bread on top of the other. This crunched the chips in between, thus completing the sandwich.

David stared at his creation, unable to move. The sandwich shouldn't have any meaning at all. It was nothing but a sandwich staring up at him as he stared back at it. He felt angry for a moment because anyone else staring at it would have felt nothing. David wanted to feel nothing. "Why did he have to be so weak?" He wanted to say to himself. "Why was he so stupid for crying over a dumb sandwich?" He wanted to believe.

He went to pick up the sandwich but couldn't touch it. There was something missing here as he stood at the counter. Sure, there was empty space around the sandwich on the plate. He could have added a side dish or maybe a drink. But the missing ingredient wasn't anything to do with the food but a certain person standing next to him. This sandwich was filled with the memory of his mother who often made it for him as he grew up. She taught him about smashing the chips in between the bread so the sandwich had additional crunch when he ate it. His memory of her was directly attached to this sandwich. His smile was never as bright as when he shared this meal with her. His mother would smile and make him laugh by dotting some mustard on each of their noses. He remembered being so little that the sandwich felt giant in his hands.

But she was gone now. And it was just a sandwich wasn't it? He wanted it to be just a sandwich. He wanted to move on from her death but couldn't. Even bringing himself to touch the sandwhich in front of him made him fear of what he would let go. Tears formed in his eyes knowing she would never come back, and he would never make more memories of the two of them eating this dumb sandwich. This made him think of who was left in his life to make new memories with. The only remaining person was his dad. A man nowhere to be found in the nothingness of his 13-year-old existence. He loathed his father and often transferred the sadness for the loss of his mother to an anger over his dad. He was a dad who cared more about his work than he did about his own son.

David wiped away his tears and walked back to the fridge. He grabbed the liquor and stared at it for a moment. It was clear and quite a large bottle. He felt he'd ignored it for too long. He cracked the bottle open and unscrewed it. Before he could think he took a quick drink and immediately spit it out in the sink behind him. The smell and taste lingered in his mouth as he tried to contain himself. The bottle was already open though, and there was no going back. He turned around and looked at the sandwich again. Staring at it, he only wished for it to go away. David took another drink.

His concentration kept him focused on swallowing the bitter sting of flavor. His eyes watered from the taste and soon fell from the pressure of his own sadness. He leaned over the counter where the sandwich sat and stared into it. But the control of its memory slowly began to loosen as he felt the effects of the liquor. He took another drink. This time the liquid didn't taste as bad knowing what to expect. He tried to stop thinking about his mother but soon his thoughts wouldn't be his own to control. The wheel was slowly taken from Tom and he wouldn't care which way his thoughts turned.

Staring at the sandwich he felt his body tingle. This was what he wanted, something to take him away from seeing the sandwich in front of him. He took another drink. The sandwich started to sway back and forth but he knew it was just his body moving side to side. He turned around leaving the sandwich behind on the cheap countertop. He slowly walked to the living room and thought maybe he was just faking the effects. He knew he was feeling something different. He sniffed and tried to hold back his tears as he took another drink of the bottle. He looked at the front door. It was dark and ominous much like the surrounding apartment. He giggled to himself thinking about his dad coming home to find him like this.

His dad would be angry to know he was not only drinking but drinking the liquor his mom purchased before she died. He started to laugh at the thought of how ridiculous it all was. His dad would probably go on some rant about death and how life is the only thing we know about. David never understood his rants about existence. Who cares after all? His dad only cared about the food he could put on David's table instead of caring about David himself. His dad fed him, clothed him, put a roof over his head, then retreated back to work or his office to write about the universe or existence. That was all the time David could ever ask of his dad. His mom was in charge of the rest. His mom was meant to be the caring and loving parent. But now she was gone, so why should David care about his dad? And if no one cared about David, why should he care about himself?

David took another drink and walked to the wall facing the living room. It was covered in family pictures. There were a few of the whole family together. Various vacations when David was too young to remember. There were a couple pictures of David and his mother on his birthday and one when they went fishing. There were a couple with just his parents. There were ones of their wedding and one on vacation before David was born. David had no pictures with his dad. David sarcastically smiled. Because having a picture of him and his dad together was too much to ask. His dad was a reclused man and a picture like that would be too embarrassing for his father to be caught smiling with his son.

David took another drink and looked at the bottle. In reality the drinks he took were not all that large but small sips taken from the bottle. Just enough to loosen David's mind and be out of his own reality. The bottle stared back at David and it made him laugh even more at the expense of his dad. It wasn't even his dad's bottle. The food in the fridge was purchased by his mom. And David's dad was much better at ordering pizza than to care about what they ate for dinner. Nothing in the apartment felt like it was his fathers at all. It was only his moms. David's negative thoughts on his father were palpable. Until he turned around at the sudden noise of the door and saw his dad standing in the front entry way.

"What the hell do you think you're doing!" Tom yelled at David as he rushed over taking the bottle out of his hand. David couldn't answer. He didn't know how to answer. His head didn't have any funnier thoughts about his dad but now went blank. He only felt his beating heart covering up pain. David's eyes once again filled with tears as he couldn't handle his dad seeing him this way.

"I'm drinking moms' liquor," David said with a giggle to try and hide the tears in his eyes. Tom quickly looked at the contents and saw that David didn't drink enough to have any horrible effect on him.

"Do you think this is funny? What would've happened if you drank too much and got drunk...?"

"Too late," David interrupted his dad smiling. Toms patience was drawing extremely thin with his son and the joke he made.

"You can't drink this! You can't use mom's death as an excuse to just do whatever you want!" Tom yelled at David attempting to drill in the seriousness of the situation.

"And who says! You? It's not even yours! Nothing in this apartment is yours! You just mooched off mom and now she's dead!" David yelled back at his father feeling the shackles of his adolescence falling away.

"What is wrong with you?" Tom said after a moment of silence. David didn't know how to reply to this question. His dad implied there was something fundamentally wrong with him as a human being for trying to escape the pain of losing his mother. David glanced to the side of his dad as to not make eye contact. What *was* wrong with him?

"I want to go back...," David said under his breath letting out a whimper of sadness. Tom, still reeling from anger, was too clouded to think about what his son meant. "...it was safe then...," David continued letting out another whimper as he stood in front of his dad.

He thought about the times his mother held him. He thought about the times his mother understood him. He thought about the times when he was shown he was loved.

"...I just want to go back," David said hoping his words would finally push through his dads incessant questioning. He hoped his dad would pick up the mantle and understand for one moment that sadness isn't the words he wrote about or the emotions he questioned in life. Sadness was a feeling he *was*... not just *in*... but *was*.

David did not feel any embrace though. He did not feel the loving parents' arms around him. He heard a sigh exit his dad's mouth. David looked back to his dad who'd now turned around and headed back to the front door.

"We'll talk about this later. I have a meeting and will be back in a couple of hours," Tom said as he opened the door still holding the bottle.

David didn't move. He continued staring at the wall

for what felt much longer than hours. His mind was blank. Time passed easily with no repercussions. He was numb. The wall didn't seem to exist and neither did anything else. Without thought, David walked towards the door and left the apartment. It was snowing outside, and the ground was covered. David didn't have a jacket but walked across the street to a park. He followed it's trails down various paths as the snow fell. His skin was wet and cold, but David continued walking.

He touched the metal railing of a large bridge crossing a river far below it. He stepped onto it and slowly walked across until he stopped in the middle to look below. He didn't think about it then and didn't expect to think of it when he stopped to look at the river.

"I just want to go back," David said standing on the edge of the bridge. Then one moment David was standing there, and the next moment he wasn't.

Tom concluded telling Kate about their sons' book and set down his own in front of her. Eric didn't say anything as he stood against the wall listening. Kate was deep in thought as Tom concluded the fate of their son's story. She didn't know how to feel. She wanted to hate the husband she just met but knew Tom told her this story to be honest with her.

"I don't know anything about existence or why I'm like this," Tom said to her. She blinked and looked at him.

"What exactly do you think you did wrong Tom?" she asked him frustrated.

"I wasn't there for my son. I needed to be there for

him," he told her feeling as though he wasn't getting the complete picture.

"That's not it, Tom," Eric chimed in suddenly.

"Shut it....," Kate said pointing at Eric. She lowered her finger and rested it on the table. "But he's right. The problem here isn't that you weren't there for your son Tom. It's only a side effect. But you know what I hear from that story?" she asked him. Tom looked at her clearly not understanding. "I hear a boy who missed his mother. It's not about you Tom. It's about a boy who desperately wanted to go back to the way things were before his mother died. Sure, you weren't there for him. We get it. Feel guilty about it. But stop thinking your sons' suicide is about you when it's not. You question what's after the curtain on a daily basis. You want to know so badly that you've clouded yourself and think it's only about your own questions forgetting that it's not about you at all," she said lecturing Tom.

"Bingo," Eric spoke up again, this time Kate allowing him to do so.

"What would you know about it?" Tom turned and asked Eric annoyed.

"I've known about David since we first met outside the Community Center," he replied.

"And you didn't think to say anything?" Tom asked.

"Again....," Eric said leaning over to Tom. "...it's not about you, is it?" he replied. It wasn't about Tom was an interesting turn for him but one not hidden. Even the man in the church spoke about his wants versus his own God's wants. The man in the churches purpose understood that existence was not about him and his wants. Tom told the story as if he were the jerk father who caused his son's suicide. The statement isn't a lie... but it isn't the truth. David's story was about David, not his father. His suicide was about a son missing his mother, and not his father.

Kate stood from her chair and started to walk away. Tom continued thinking about the lessons he was just shared. "Eric and I will be at your parents. Meet us there if you're ever ready," she said walking away. Realizing what Kate meant, Eric left the wall and followed her leaving Tom alone.

Chapter XIX

A Talk in front of Darkness

"What was it? Why did you ignore him?" Lindsey asked. She broke hours of silence lingering between the two of them as they sat in the grass directly in front of the curtain. This time, Tom and Lindsey sat facing outwards away from the curtain. After their embraced hug the two of them were silent for a long time but neither of them did not want to look at the curtain. Instead, they watched people come and go. They watched people who were clearly in a state of trance as they walked into the curtain, but neither of them watched the act itself. They watched the family members and friends who came to say goodbye to their loved ones leaving existence. The entirety of the Community Centers focus lead to the curtain. Every hallway, corridor, and room pointed in some form to the center of the Community Center where the curtain hung. And yet, Tom and Lindsey sat looking away from it. They'd had their fill of being close to it hours prior. A terrifying night where Tom was almost thrown through the curtain by Lindsey.

Tom focused on the different people. Everyone unique and from a different part of existence. Every one of them with the same ballot stuffed in their pockets scribbled with different answers. He saw Christian families of different denominations mourning the loss of loved ones. He saw one woman held a cross to her lips with soft prayers breathing from her mouth. The cross, Tom thought, was much like the puzzle piece people held onto closely. A belief attached to the cross, but it had no weight in of itself. Some family's beliefs had them singing songs as they sent their loved ones beyond the curtain. Songs of hope and faith to help comfort the ones still existing. Of course there were the normal emotions blanketing every person. Anger and sadness were the dominant feelings and occasionally individuals who were uncontrollably laughing. It was clear to Tom these people didn't laugh from disrespect of the ones going beyond, but out of a way to relieve the pain in themselves.

He also noticed practices of varying beliefs unfold in a spectacular fashion. He saw one person setting up a small altar. It was a wooden box with steps to its top where incense was burned. Red and yellow powder splashed across its surface and in the center sat a small statue of a blue god. It was a beautiful work of art meant to represent this person's god. Pieces of fruit were spread in front of the small statue as a form of offering to the god. The person then bent a knee and prayed for his loved one. He saw a woman then walk from one of the corridors with a bottle of whiskey in her hand. She looked like a rough and spirited woman but unbroken by the man who was leaving her. She unscrewed the top of the bottle and poured a bit on the grass in front of her. Multitudes of beliefs were presented constantly to the curtain but most of them were comforts for people performing the theatrics.

Lindsey on the other hand studied the structure of the Community Center itself. Its stones were a mixture of old and new. On the bottom of the wall were large stones laid down but exceptionally smooth as if it were placed just the day before. On top of this stone was a cracked and beaten one. Vines and mold grew around it looking as if it were thousands of years old. This stone was followed by a brand-new stone. The walls of the Community Center all looked similar to this one. It was a mixture of old and new as if someone from thousands of years ago laid one stone, followed by someone just today, and followed again by someone thousands of years ago. This was not a surprise to Lindsey who preferred the first floor than that of the second. She was very aware of the inconsistency of time and how it affected the first floor. The park they sat in looked only like a continuation of the forest outside the Community Center. The first ones to exist decided to build the construction around this particular spot. Then again, the structure itself was a constant construction by those across time.

She thought heavily on this to keep her mind away from understanding the deep turmoil she pushed herself through just hours earlier. She tried to ignore her dark actions to push Tom through the curtain but couldn't hide from them forever. The silence between the two of them was not an eternal bliss they would enjoy. After finishing Toms book she didn't understand how she was supposed to forgive him. But there in his pages read that Tom would live to see another day after she tried to murder him. The two of them not only connected emotionally through guilt and forgiveness but found the semblance of friendship through the grief and time.

Following the book, she did as time wanted. But more importantly she didn't understand how she would ever know if she actually did forgive him. Yes she thought the words of forgiveness. But the anger and hurt she had would rise and fall with every passing minute. If she only knew, Toms guilt rose and fell almost in unison. Forgiveness isn't hard because we can't think it. Forgiveness is hard because it's not a singular act. Guilt does not disappear the first time someone forgives. Forgiveness is only a step. It is only the spark of light. It's enough to fan a flame but needs to be nurtured by both parties involved to catch fire.

"I don't know. Ever since I arrived here...," Tom paused almost turning to look at the curtain but catching himself and looked outward again. "...all I've been able to think about is the curtain....," Tom continued. Just at the edge of the park they both saw a long golden line touch the top of the where the dome sat. The morning sun peaked high above the Community Center and began illuminating the field of green.

"But shouldn't *you* know? You're the one who finished my book," he asked her.

"Those books are not windows to our souls. They're windows to our lives," she told Tom almost scoffing that he didn't understand. "Sorry, I'm still processing this," she caught herself. Tom didn't say anything at first but stared at the grass. He thought about when he watched David go behind the curtain. How he did nothing because he didn't know what existence was. He felt pain when David left his eyesight but didn't know why. It was as if there was a natural force telling him the curtain was bad in the practice David used it.

"It's the same reason I ignore my own book I guess," Tom said turning his head and looking at the unopened text sitting next to him. "Anything to keep me from having to deal with the reality in front of me," Tom said continuing to look at the book.

"What reality in front of you? You created the terrible reality for you and your son. It's on you," she said. At this, Tom was a bit surprised at her accusation. Not because she snapped at him, but because she didn't know the full story as he suspected.

"I'm talking about my wife....," he said to her solemnly. Her attention was grabbed as she looked at him. "Months before David, she passed away," he said to her.

"I didn't...," she started to say then quietly stopped.

"I know. But the reality of losing her was something I couldn't handle and seeing him was a reminder every day that she was gone. I ignored him. I ignored his needs. And I've never been smart at much of anything. School, work, family, and friends were always so confusing to me. So instead of trying to interact and become a better person I just stare at the curtain. I get lost in the thoughts of what could happen on the other side to the point where I ignored my son and myself," Tom said still staring at the book. He turned his back and watched the grass as sunlight seeped between the blades.

"We all have our escape I suppose. Yours is just the one thing most people try to ignore," she told Tom almost laughing at the irony.

"You're saying it's the same as if I drank heavily or found some other outlet for my fears?" he asked her as she nodded her head.

"I don't know how I'll ever finish my book," Tom said feeling defeated. But this was not a strange feeling to him any more than staring at the curtain was strange for him. The guilt rose again in his being even if he knew he was forgiven.

"I didn't think there was any way I wouldn't have thrown you through the curtain last night," Lindsey said shrugging her shoulders.

"Why didn't you? You have every right to," Tom replied letting the guilt overpower him.

"Because it isn't *my* truth. Your book isn't finished Tom. And for whatever reason, I'm not the end of you. But I do know how your story ends. You'll finish it. I have no doubt," she told him.

"That's very kind of you to say," he said to her. Picking up his book he held it in front of him with a loud sigh. He looked at its cover and thought about the journey he'd taken this far. Meeting Eric and Kate was only the beginning. Clive was especially an interesting character and he wondered where that mysterious man had gone.

"What do you know about evil?" he asked her suddenly after a moment.

"Evil? What about it?" she asked raising and eyebrow.

"I made a promise to a friend of mine. If he showed me the second floor then he wanted me to meet evil," he said. Lindsey laughed at this idea.

"You don't know what I believe do you?" she said through her laughter. Tom widened his eyes and realized he actually had no idea what she believed. This was odd because Tom often wanted to know what people's personal beliefs were and here he sat with someone who actually almost ended his existence and didn't know what they checked on the ballot.

"I believe in existence...," she said standing up abruptly and looking to the dome high above them. "...I believe in what we are right now. We are created by the forest and to the forest we will return...," Lindsey said stretching out her arms and gesturing towards the forest beyond the Community Center walls. Tom was taken back slightly but her belief matched the spontaneous look she had. "...evil doesn't 'exist' the way we know it. You can't just waltz into a room and sit down with it. Everything has its place and this place is everything," she said smiling and twirling slowly around. Tom didn't know about this belief.

"What is evil?" Tom asked interrupting her spontaneous dance.

"What do you mean?" she asked still twirling and smiling. She closed her eyes and let the sunshine touch her face. She was happy to be talking about her belief and not something as dark as David's death.

"I mean, I don't know what that word 'evil' means," he told her. She stopped twirling around a moment and raised an eyebrow thinking about how to answer it.

"Evil is the word men gave to anything that isn't *their* truth," she said.

"I don't agree with David going behind the curtain. So that was evil?" he asked her bringing the conversation back to the dark areas she did not want to explore.

"To you and me, yes it is," she told him. Tom felt like Lindsey was trying to be wise like Clive, but she came across as someone who knew all the answers instead.

"Who agrees for David to go behind the curtain?" he asked her.

"David did. Evil and suffering are only illusions of the mind. We must learn to control these illusions, or we will lose ourselves to them," she said to him sitting back down.

"So, because no one else felt the pain David felt, it's only an illusion for him to have to conquer?" Tom asked her. She wasn't as happy with his analogy. "Is that why you didn't throw me behind the curtain? Because the pain you felt you understood to be an illusion to conquer?" he continued asking his questions not meaning to tear apart her belief. She thought for a moment about his questions.

"Tom, we are our own gods. We wrote the books. We write what 'evil' is in the books. We return to the forest and reemerge new beings," she told him fed up with his questions. Tom remembered a similar interaction with the Captain where he suggested they were all individual gods writing their own stories. But the Captain sounded adamant to suggest this were untrue.

"You don't believe I'll ever be able to meet evil?" Tom asked her ignoring her core beliefs.

"There are legends a third floor to the Community Center exists. But only stories passed between the souls to explain the illusions we create for ourselves," she told Tom. He didn't really want to believe what she said as it would make Clive a liar. Then again, Tom never associated evil with Christianity. Evil was something plaguing every belief and every person.

Tom stood up from the grass and brushed off his pants. "I made a promise to a friend of mine. If he showed me the second floor then he wanted me to meet evil," he said. Lindsey started laughing again at this idea.

"You won't find anything. It's a story told to new

people of the Community Center. Evil and his game," she told him.

"Game?" Tom asked curious about what she meant.

"Oh yes, the game that would end all evil for the ones on the first floor. If you beat evil then nothing bad would ever happen again. No matter the individual, everything would be good," she told him as she looked up. Tom picked up his book and looked down at it, knowing Clive was the reason he was able to understand things at least a little bit more.

"What's the game?" he asked. Lindsey stopped laughing and sighed. She thought this conversation was becoming trivial with childish stories.

"You must play the game. No one knows exactly what the third floor looks like because based on legend it changes for everyone. Basically, everything on the first floor represents something on the second floor. You represent someone in that book...," she said pointing at Tom's book. "...the walls of the Community Center, the curtain, the forest outside, they all represent something on the second floor...," she said gesturing to all the different things surrounding them. "But the challenge... is guessing what evil represents on the second floor. What in your own book and every other book does evil represent? What is it a reflection of in that world?" she asked Tom. "Then you must tell evil why you believe it shouldn't be allowed to exist in the first place. It will argue with you and you will argue back. It's a debate going deep into philosophy. The story goes that most never return," she said with an ominous tone. She was only joking but Tom could feel his fear growing.

"Never return?" Tom pressed. Lindsey stood up next to Tom.

"It's a deep conversation you will get lost in until your mind is ripped apart...," she told Tom smiling. "... that is... if it's real. But like I told you before, evil only exists because we make it exists with our minds," she said pointing at her head and pointing at his. Secretly Tom hoped this were true. Maybe evil was just a misunderstanding of the pages of his book. But he didn't understand why he still felt guilty if he knew this truth. If evil didn't exist then he could conquer it and not deal with the consequences evil presented.

"Thank you Lindsey," Tom said to her.

"For what? I almost threw you in the curtain last night," she said laughing slightly.

"According to you, that's just *your* truth. Thank you for showing me forgiveness when we were both only in darkness," he replied. She stopped giggled and smiled at him. If evil didn't exist, then how could her forgiveness exist? Maybe forgiveness was empty just like his guilt.

"What will you do now?" she asked him.

"I'm going to visit my parents. I think maybe they can help me with my book," Tom said as he started to walk away.

"Tom be safe," she told him as he walked up the hill towards one of the corridors emptying into the park.

Chapter XX

Finishing a Book

I bet you're a little confused. We've jumped around from different Tom's and different time's in Tom's existence but acting as they're happening one after the other or at the same time. I told you from the beginning time works differently on the first floor. Tom, who just met his wife, and Tom, who just finished talking to Lindsey are now both headed to his parents' house. But how can this be when they are two separate timelines? Every story you read you make a sacrifice to reality in believing something unrealistic. Whether you're reading a historical fiction or a science fiction novel, there are elements of reality you give up in order to transport yourself to this new reality. I ask nothing new of you. The only thing I ask is for you to sacrifice the linear idea you have of "time". Because whether you wish it to be true or not, once you nullify time (in any story), you are in new territory.

These two Tom's are not two separate timelines at all. They are the same time, and they are the same Tom. Tom will walk to his parent's house from both his wife and from Lindsey. He will walk into his parent's house again but now with the knowledge of both experiences and even the experience of the church. Drat, I forgot about the third Tom in the church.

Want to be even more confused? Tom in the church hasn't left yet. And yet the Tom who meets with his parents in this chapter will have the knowledge of Tom who met his wife, Tom who met Lindsey, and Tom in the church even though he never left the church. Why? Because time is not a straight line nor is it a jumbled line. Time is an alphabet of letters ready to explain a story in any structure it can find. It is not the river running down a mountain, it is the water breaking over rocks while also sitting still in the lake. And from this position you should be able to conclude there isn't just three Tom's either. There's hundreds of him throughout the Community Center collectively equaling a lifetime in his book. But we won't go into detail of everyone, only the events to complete the story in front of us.

Me? I know I haven't spoken up much. That's because Tom's emotion and questions crowd the space in this book quite a lot. It was easier in the beginning when his questions were simple. They were not bombarded by the answers other people give him only creating false truths or even more questions. They were a framework for who he was. What's after the curtain? Which belief is right? Although these questions still exist in his mind they are plagued by what other people's inputs are. What's after the curtain but also why does it matter? Which belief is right but also we need to live in the moment... don't we? Adults ask questions to prove something. They want to prove their belief to be right. They want to prove God is real or fake to reinforce their own way to enlightenment. But children? Children ask questions only to know. What's after the curtain? Which belief is right? They don't want to know because it proves any argument they have for themselves. Children ask questions because they know the answer they currently have (nothing) is wrong and they want to know what is right. They know what they want is wrong... and something else external from what they already know has to be right.

Tom's obsession over the questions make it a little difficult for me to squeeze my two cents in. It isn't because I'm not there. If there are words on a page then I'm there. Tom feels a heavy guilt on his shoulders for David's death and Lindsey "forgave" the only way she knew how. By... not killing him. Seems like the bare minimum action if you ask me but hey, forgiveness looks like many things. But does one's forgiveness eliminate one's guilt? If it should but still doesn't... what does the guilty person do? Who has ultimate control, not over what you can do with forgiveness, but what you can do with your own guilt?

Maybe Lindsey was right about evil being an illusion. Wouldn't that mean Tom's guilt is an illusion? Tom's guilt is only something he needs to understand is fake in order to be better. Maybe if he only meditated a bit and travelled to view different perspectives of reality this would eliminate his guilt. But then Tom is only doing one thing and that's to get rid of his guilt. Isn't that inherently selfish? And besides, you and I both know Tom would say something like "It doesn't matter, we're all still on this side of the curtain." And as long as we are, guilt could be morally good and what we think is good could actually be evil.

By this standard the evil on the third floor could only be perceived evil. Changing the perception would change it to be inherently good. That's only if we know what good and evil actually are and as long as Tom is on this side of the curtain, he believes there is no way to actually know. He was interested in meeting evil on the third floor. He kept his excitement slightly hidden as to not show he was interested in understanding it. But he did make a promise to his friend, Clive, and said he would meet this thing called evil. I'm up there all the time, I don't see what the big deal is personally.

What do I mean I'm up there all the time? I'm fairly certain I've explained this already. But chapter three is still existing even if you're not reading it. Meaning I'm still on the third floor. The words are still printed in that chapter and every other chapter also. The beginning and the end are all happening, and I'm interwoven between them all. There is no power nor weakness of this book I am not found. The story is separate from me, but I am the story.

Oh! We did find out more about the sandwich I spoke about in the first chapter! I know there's a lot surrounding the sandwich that makes it so much more. But it is a pretty classic sandwich.

Where's Clive been? Wasn't he supposed to be waiting for Tom when he came back? Apparently not. Clive had an appointment he needed to attend a long with Kate and Eric. All three of them actually were at Tom's parents' house. Clive and Kate inside speaking with his parents while Eric stood outside smoking a cigarette. He stood against the brick wall connected to the front door. The hanging garden swings slightly in the window. Eric wore a straight black suit with a black tie. He stared downward at the ground not expecting to be interrupted by any person until Tom found himself standing in front of him. Eric looked up from the ground in frustration.

"Honestly, I'm surprised you showed," he said to Tom who was not nearly as well dressed as Eric. Tom stood bewildered by the sudden aggressive tone of Eric.

"What do you mean?" he asked him. Eric shook his head as he put his cigarette out on the bottom of his shoe.

"You know I always knew you were obsessed with your books and the second floor. But never so obsessed to forget about your own son's memorial," Eric scoffed. Tom was dumbfounded by what he'd just learned. The guilt Tom faced was ever present. Not finishing his book was showing him how much he was missing.

"I didn't know. I...," Tom tried to think of an excuse for not being here.

"You didn't know because you're too scared of your own life. How can you care for anyone else when you don't care about your own book?" Eric spat out at his friend. He didn't even know if it was something he believed. Eric only wanted to tear down Tom for not being at his son's memorial service. Tom looked down at his book and realized not finishing it was going to write itself into more problems.

"I'm not a good person Eric, I know. Is that what you want me to say?" Tom asked him defensively.

"Tom we know! We know you're not a good person! You don't have to reiterate that like it's some sad story for you to manipulate us with!" Eric yelled at Tom as he grasped the handle of the front door. He pressed his forehead against the red wood and sighed.

"We want you to finish your book, Tom. We want you to not be so afraid of life and the curtain to the point where you only question and stop moving forward," Eric said closing his eyes. For the first time Tom saw Eric as more than the belief he put on his ballot. Eric was dressed up for a memorial that was most likely Christian. Eric put his beliefs aside and spoke to Tom as if they were equals in not understanding existence.

"You're not a good person Tom. But it's not your actions that make you bad. It's your stagnation and refusal to move forward making you a bad person," Eric said opening his eyes and concluding what he said. He opened the door and walked inside. Tom stood in the doorway wondering if it would ever close. Eric, for a moment, thought about shutting it. But he looked at Tom and saw only a person who made mistakes. Eric looked to his left where a hallway mirror hung reflecting himself to be the same person who also made mistakes. Tom, still in the doorway, never saw it close. He was allowed to enter at any time whether he was late or not.

"When you're ready," Eric calmly told Tom. He turned and walked into the living room exiting Tom's view. Tom could just barely hear the sound of people speaking with one another and thought he heard someone crying slightly.

Looking down at his book again he knew he had a lot to cover before he could face what was inside the house. The last thing he read in his own book was that of his wife dying. The last thing he read in his own book was him ignoring his family and being obsessed with the questions flooding his mind. Tom sat down against the brick wall and continued staring at the cover of his book. He was told constantly that this wasn't about him and yet he had to finish his book in order to progress. There was no way to face the memorial of his son without understanding who he was as a person and being better because of it.

Better... Tom smiled at the idea. He didn't know what it meant. Better than what he is? What if he read his book and he was only worse? Would he be better or worse by his own perception, by the perception of others, or by an objective truth of the universe? Better. Clive wanted Tom to meet the embodiment of evil represented in this world and living throughout the books on the first floor. But how could he do that if he wasn't positive what evil was to begin with? Was evil actually good and was good actually evil? Tom found himself going in circles of the questions he wrote about instead of finishing his book once again.

Tom stopped thinking. He cracked open the cover to his book and flipped to the page he finished last. The page where he found his wife had passed away. Turning the page to the next chapter his heart experienced pain as he read the chapter title. He knew the next chapter was supposed to be about his son. The next chapters would be about David taking his own life. But that's not what the chapter was about. The chapter title, printed in beautiful calligraphy, chapter fourteen of Thomas Lewis's book was titled "Me".

Tom gripped the book tighter as he knew what kind of man he would read about. The first line of the chapter only helped reenforce the negativity of who Thomas Lewis really was and why Eric was so upset with him. "What is after death?" the first line read. The chapter only continued into self-defeating questions about the nature of death and what was in the afterlife. What was his wife experiencing and how could anyone ever truly know what was after death?

Tom continued to read word after word and only gripped the book tighter and tighter wanting every second to throw it against the ground and leave everything he was behind. This man in the book deserved nothing more than to be burned and never read again. There wasn't a single paragraph about Tom's son or wondering how he was doing, only question after question. Finishing chapter fourteen of his own book convinced Tom there was no hope for himself. He turned the page to chapter fifteen. The title was something unexpected. His hands loosened on the front and back cover of the book. The title read "You".

The chapter started out just like chapter fourteen with questions and useless knowledge of philosophy and theology. Constant annoyance and anger being thrown around as if Tom was the only one to ever ask such questions; only to be interrupted by sudden dialogue of his best friend and a realization of where he was; standing at the funeral of his son as they lowered David into the ground. But Tom was not standing near the casket or near the family members. No, Tom stood next to his car wearing a nice suit just as Eric did next to him.

"Your son is dead, Tom," Eric said solemnly. Tom wiped tears away from his eyes.

Something Tom didn't even know was there until it was written.

"Kate is dead, Tom," Eric continued stating the fact. Tom looked at his best friend as if he'd just been stabbed in the back not realizing what Eric was doing.

"Yeah? Like I don't know?" Tom said angrily.

"Do you? You're so focused on where they've gone

you forget to tell yourself that they *are* gone. Tom, they are gone," Eric said rudely. Tom grabbed Eric's jacket forcefully bringing him closer.

"Say it again. Say it like you know who I am, Eric. After all you apparently do," he said in a shaky and nervous voice. Eric didn't fight back or get violent. He held onto Tom's wrists and looked him in the eyes.

"It's not about you Tom. It's not about what you know or don't know about existence or the afterlife," Eric said softly. Tom started to tear up and cry at the sound of his best friends confronting yet comforting voice. Tom's fists released him, and he lowered his head staring at the dirt where he believed he belonged.

"It's about both of them Tom," Eric said pointing to the funeral going on behind them. Tom continued staring at the dirt. Where he believed he belonged for all of his misdeeds. But this wasn't about him or where he belonged. It wasn't about whether or not he was going to hell after death or even where his own family ended up after death. He looked up from the dirt and saw the funeral. So many people coming to see the death of his son buried next to his late wife. That's what mattered; not Tom, not his ballot, not the curtain, but it was others that mattered and what could be done for them.

Eric placed a hand on Toms back as they both slowly walked back to the funeral where everyone stood. Tom saw the closed casket lower into the ground. He stood at the front until every person had left. Now he stared at the tombstone of his son next to his wife. Eric, his parents, and an old professor named Clive paid their condolences and left Tom alone to view the missing parts of his soul. Questions filled the gaps between these never-ending spaces. The problem wasn't his questions. Tom's problem was his attempt to fill the void in his soul with the questions. He wasn't going to know what happens after death and wasn't even sure he would know upon actually dying. But it wasn't about Tom. The chapters of these books were about the lives surrounding him and what he did for others.

He could hear the sound of nature around the cemetery. Beautiful green grass and a small wind blew through the leaves as he slowly came to this realization. Tom took a deep breath and walked away from the gravestones. The chapter ended with Tom reading about and understanding something crucial which was not to let questions take over his life, understanding it isn't about questioning, and that his existence was only there to work for the betterment of others. He wanted to think about how his guilt could have swayed him to do better earlier in the book or how he should have done certain things differently. But he didn't. And it was written this way. It would never change but the next chapters could help him have a book finished with someone who did his best to help others.

Tom continued reading about this character in another world. There were still questions even in the next chapter, but they did not control his actions to the point of forgetting where he was or why he was there. Tom in the book started to focus much more on his work but always with the underlining conviction to help. He started talking to people who were homeless and offering food and shelter to those in need. Anonymously doing his best to help others any way he could based on the knowledge that existence would never be about what he wanted but what he could do for others. A recurring motto for Tom in the book became "I have a beating heart, two working hands, and two working lungs. I can do something to help someone... anyone." It was a simple mantra Tom in the book repeated to himself any time he got nervous about starting a new project. Politics, the economy, and the world would all change and move to different paths but in any situation Tom wanted to be working towards what he could do for others.

The last chapter of Tom's book was titled "Into the Unknown". Tom read the chapter and closed the book sitting in front of his parent's house. He knew how he would die (at least in the book). Tom knew where he belonged based on past actions of ignoring his wife and son only to have them both die. He flooded his own thoughts and everyone he knew with questions no one could possibly have the answer to. But he wasn't going to represent that man. Tom in the Community Center represented a man who only wanted to forfeit what he wanted for what he could do for others.

He stood up from the ground and looked at the red open door of his parents' house. Hours had passed as he sat in the front but knew it'd only been a few minutes since Eric walked inside. The door was still open for him to walk in and see his family. He needed to be there for them. That's the man he wanted to represent. He walked into the house and shut the door behind him. Walking around the corner he saw his parents standing near the kitchen door. His father's hand on his mother's back as she blew her nose from tears. Kate stood next to Clive as they both stopped talking and looked at Tom. Eric stood next to a mantle with greenery and a picture of David looking out at the room. Kate smiled and slowly walked over to Tom.

"You're always welcome home," she whispered to him as she wrapped her arms around him. Tom held onto her and comforted his wife.

Chapter XXI

Wake and Wander

"You look tired," Tom's mother said as they sat at the kitchen table. Tom remembered this seat well. It was where he first learned about the second floor only days prior. He sat attempting to relax with his hand on a coffee cup. His mother poured him hot chocolate while she sipped on coffee. His thumb circled the cups porcelain edge as he thought about the experiences he encountered. It'd only been a few days to him and yet he was now almost the age his parents were at the time he first met them. Time was moving more rapidly with every passing experience and he felt as though he was either missing out on events or he never had the chance to experience them in the first place. Although Tom learned a lot in his prior days he still understood so little. He wanted to do right by others and be selfless. His book sat on the table, but it felt far away as he tried not to focus on himself anymore.

"I am tired," he finally told his mother, breaking the silence she knew would be inevitable in these moments. His mother looked much older than previous days when he first met her. She carried wisdom in her eyes masking the pain of losing her grandchild.

"It's okay to question things Tom. I hope you know it was never anyone's intent to keep you from it," she spoke with shaken words. Tom continued staring at his thumb circling the side of the cup.

"I know, Mom. It's just...," Tom tried to think of what he wanted to say but no words would form. The memorial for his son was a nice way to remember him by. But he deeply wanted to understand why anything like this would happen in the first place.

"No person should have to see their child walk through the curtain," his mother said. This line was nothing new to him. It was something various people in the Community Center said about ones who committed suicide. Whispers one could hear in the park about what should have happened and what shouldn't have happened. But now, when he heard it from someone he knew, he felt a bitterness to the mantra.

"No person should have to see their own child *choose* to go through the curtain either," he said with growing frustration staring at his thumb still rotating. The disassociating from his mother only watered the frustration in his mind. She wasn't surprised by his distaste for any sort of help. She'd been through a lot herself and knew he was going to be hateful for a while.

"It's only the nature of the soul to fight against reality," she said to him sipping on her cup of coffee. But this didn't satisfy his question.

"And when did David fight?!" Tom raised his voice at his mother slamming his palm against the table. His cup of hot chocolate and book shook slightly dripping some onto the table. His father peered into the entrance from the living room to make sure everything was okay. He saw Tom sitting in his chair, palm flat on the table, staring hatefully but curiously into his mother's eyes. Her eyes were compassionate. In her age she knew there was no more time for anger. His father turned his head back into the living room not wanting to be involved with the situation.

"When did David fight to stay on this side of the curtain? When did David's soul look at the curtain and turn away or at least try?" Tom pressed his mother. She didn't waver in any action she made. She slowly sat her coffee back onto the table and Tom continued staring at her. Tom's mother knew Tom had to have these conversations and experience the beating heart of hatred. She knew the only way to climb out of sorrow and despair was through a long and hard journey of grief no mother wanted to see her own child witness.

"How do you know he didn't fight?" she asked him. Tom continued staring at her inciting any form of fight he could. He desperately wanted to relieve the energy building inside himself. He knew deep down her conflicting anger would never come.

"He walked right through the curtain mom! I was right there!" Tom yelled at his mother again. Heads raised in the living room at the muffled sound of Tom yelling in the kitchen. Kate tried to ignore the ongoing conflict. She stared at the ground and focused on her futile attempts to keep from crying.

"And walking through the curtain is giving up?" Tom's mother pressed back against his anger. "You said yourself you don't know what's beyond the curtain. But you're claiming to know that if someone doesn't fight going through it then they gave up," she continued. The intensity in her voice was not of anger but of forcing Tom to think deeper instead of shying away from his questions.

"And what exactly did David give up, Tom? By your standards he gave up a reality he didn't even know existed or not," she concluded with a deep breath. Eric's ears pricked at what he heard Tom's mother say from the living room. Being an atheist, Eric believed there was nothing after death. This was the only way to exist in any form from Eric's perception. But Tom claimed he didn't know what he believed. So why did Tom feel anything at all when David walked through the curtain?

"We don't know what's behind the curtain mom. David decided to explore that part of existence on his own...," Tom said lowering his voice. He couldn't see from the cloud of anger, but his mother was forcing him to dig deeper into the questions surrounding his mind. "...he could be burning in hell. He could be in heaven. He could be experiencing an infinite number of different outcomes," Tom said as if this was one of the reasons he was sad for his sons passing. As if not knowing what's after the curtain was the only reason to mourn the loss of his son.

"Then why don't you go through then?" Tom's mother asked suddenly. "Why don't you follow in your son's footsteps and walk through the curtain? Explore with him. See what's on the others side Tom," she said. Eric grinned at what he heard from the living room. He remembered sitting across from Tom being asked the same question. Tom remembered this as well and replied similarly to the way Eric did.

"To experience this right now. There's lots in the Community Center to live for," Tom shot back.

"That's a nothing answer for people who don't seek," she rebutted quicker than he intended. Eric and Tom both were stunned at her accusation. "Your son is gone, and you sit here telling me the reason you won't follow him into the unknown is because you like chicken fingers?" she continued. "You can do better than that Tom," his mother concluded picking her cup of coffee up and taking a drink.

Tom's hand relaxed on the table as he put more effort into why he never chose to just simply walk through the curtain. Every person in the house had their reasons whether it was a religious belief or an atheistic belief. But Tom? Tom didn't know what he believed. Why did Tom not walk through the curtain? Afterall if he didn't know the answer to the question then there was no reason not to leave the house and walk through.

"If I have no reason to live... I have no reason to die," Tom whispered after a moment of silence. His mother was a little surprised to hear terminology used on the second floor. This answer did not appease her arguments though. She sat her cup down and although Eric (overhearing the conversation) was satisfied with his answer, Tom's mother was not.

"So you create a scale," she answered Tom. His eyes shot back to his mother.

"How so?" he asked.

"Once you have a reason to live then you have less chance in having a reason to die, no?" she asked him. Tom thought about it for a moment and saw the scale beginning to form. He nodded his head at her in agreement.

"It works the other way, as most scales do. When you have a reason to die, you have less reason to live. And right now, according to your own disbelief, the scale is in favor of death," she told him sternly. Tom realized she was right. With David's suicide Tom only had a reason to go beyond the curtain and less reason to remain alive. He had his reason to walk through the curtain to find his son but no reason to stay.

"And yet...," his mother whispered. "...here you are. So, Tom, why is that?" she asked. Tom processed what she said. He had to seriously consider why (if he truly didn't believe anything) he remained on this side of the curtain. Why did he fear when he stepped so close to it? Because it would end his being? But he didn't know if it would end his being. Did he fear the curtain because he knew he could never come back? Maybe he was able to come back and stepping through would make him realize this. Tom didn't believe anything because every belief was as equally possible as the next. And now Tom not only had no belief, but he had at least one reason to walk through the curtain... his son. Now Tom had to ask himself, why was he sitting with his mom instead of walking through?

"I don't know," Tom finally said breaking his thoughts. His mom smiled.

"Sure you do," she said to him.

"Because God is real, and I fear the reality of hell? Is that what you're going to say?" he said somewhat sarcastically to her.

"Of course not. All of us here know why," she said looking to the entry way of the kitchen. Tom's father, Clive, Kate, and Eric all stood looking at the two of them.

"It's why I'm your best friend," Eric said as he leaned against the counter.

"The reason you're still on this side of the curtain is the reason I knew you would be okay on the second floor," Tom's father said with a beating pride for his son.

"It's why I fell in love with you," Kate quietly said trying to keep her composure. She stood in the corner almost in darkness, rubbing her arm, feeling crowded.

"And it's why you're going to the third floor with

me," Clive said. This comment silenced everyone in the room except for Tom's mother. She suddenly gasped.

"No one said anything about going to the third floor? What are you talking about?" Tom's mother spoke at hearing this for the first time. Tom looked back to his mother.

"I promised Clive I would go to the third floor if he took me to the second. I don't even know what it is," Tom said to his mother trying to comfort her.

"You can't do that Tom. No," she said frantically. Tom looked a little confused at her refusal of him going.

"I don't even know what it is? I've talked to some people who think it doesn't even exist," Tom said still trying to calm her down. His mother stood up from the table and wrapped her arms around him.

"You can't go. Promise me you won't go," she said worriedly. Her sudden display of emotion was surprising to everyone. "I promise we won't argue anymore. I promise, just stay here instead," she said with a shake in her voice.

"He has to go," Kate said under her breath and staring at the ground. She'd been quiet most the day with people giving their condolences to her but never had she felt more alone.

"Kate?" Tom asked softly as his eyes looked at her. She didn't think much about the events taking place. But she knew if Tom met evil then she could have answers of her own. "I need to talk to Kate...," Tom said looking around at everyone in the kitchen. He looked at his mother who'd now stepped back to look at Tom.

"...privately," he said to her. His mother, with tears in her eyes, wiped them away and ushered everyone out of the kitchen. Tom and Kate hadn't been alone since he told her what would happen to their son. But now, it happened, and the irony was she stood in the memorial knowing she would pass away before her own son. She continued looking down at the floor rubbing her right arm. Tom stood and walked in front of her. She didn't move and he didn't attempt to embrace her.

"When you told me the story of David... it was just a story...," she said under her breath unable to look at Tom. "I blamed myself in that moment for passing away. I blamed you. I blamed everything I could find. But... now it's real... it's the most real I've ever felt...," she said trying to piece together what she had to say. "I've never felt much like the person in my own book until now when I'm experiencing his passing. I don't know where God is... I don't know where the God I worship is...," she continued letting out small breaths of tears. "... Tom I can't find the good in this evil," she said breaking the wall keeping her from crying.

She wrapped her arms around Tom and buried her face into his chest letting every tear run. Tom held her close and didn't let go. He thought about the flip side of the coin in the books. Kate lost her life to cancer and as a result David committed suicide. Here in the Community Center, David committed suicide and Kate was experiencing this pain. She'd read her own book and knew about David, but never knew about the suicide since her book ended earlier than his.

"God's here," Tom said softly as she held onto him. Words he didn't expect to say but they came flowing from his mouth anyway. He didn't even know which god he spoke about. Kate opened her eyes with her forehead still against his chest. She hadn't expected her husband to say this either. Tom had no idea what he believed and yet he said those words with conviction as if he knew.

"You said you don't know what evil is," Kate said looking up at him. Rivers of tears poured from her eyes, but she kept composure. "And no one's given you an answer yet," she continued. "Evil is what took our son away. It's what forced our son to go beyond the curtain on his own choice," she said letting go of him. She walked past him to the kitchen table and put her hand on it. "I don't know where God is Tom, and you say he's here even in this evil," she said sniffing. "Show me. Go to the third floor and show me there is still good even in this place," she told him.

A heart of vengeance burned inside of her. But revenge was not on her mind, she used this passionate rage to seek out goodness. She turned her head to see Tom looking at her with urgent eyes. He nodded his head and walked to her. Kissing her, he turned away, and walked to the living room where the others were. Kate walked behind him and leaned against the entry way to the living room.

Tom's mother sat on a small bench with his father's

hand on her back trying to comfort her. Eric and Clive stood next to each other waiting for Tom to explain what would happen.

"I'm going to the third floor," Tom said. His mother let out a small burst of crying. He walked to her first and got on one knee. They looked at each other closely.

"I have to do this mom. I can't explain why but this is my path just like it was David's story. If evil exists... then good does also. I'm going to find good in this evil. Trust me," he said to her. Barely keeping her composure she nodded her head as she wrapped her arms around him. Standing up Tom turned to his father.

"You were right. Time is very addictive. I was stuck thinking it was all about me when in the end it's what I can do for others instead," he told him. His father smiled.

"Yeah, it's a pretty addictive part of time. It's hard to break but I knew you could," his dad chuckled as they gave each other a hug. Tom looked around the living room for Eric but didn't see him.

"Outside," Tom's mother said to him trying to help at least one last time. Clive walked to the front door followed by Tom. He looked back at his wife and grinned. She smiled at him and knew he would find the answer. The two men walked outside to see Eric smoking a cigarette.

"I'm going to the third floor," Tom told him. Eric inhaled his cigarette and took it out of his mouth.

"I know. Things will be different when you get back.

It'll change a lot of things," he said to him. Tom was under the impression Eric meant he thought Tom could actually succeed in ridding evil from the Community Center. Tom didn't go to the third floor for this reason though. Tom didn't care much for evil, but he wanted to find the good in it. He had to show Kate where God was in this evil.

"It'll be alright," Tom said giving Eric a hug.

"I know buddy. When you come back, remember one thing for me," Eric said. Tom looked a little confused but nodded his head. "Remember... time works differently on the first floor," he said to Tom.

"I think I've been here long enough to know that?" Tom said a little confused.

"You're right," Eric said grinning. "Just promise me," he said with serious intent. Tom didn't understand, but he agreed with the terms. Eric put his cigarette out on his shoe and gestured down the hall for the two to walk away. They both did and Eric walked back inside.

Chapter XXII

A Child finds Evil

"Where is the entrance to the third floor?" Tom asked Clive as they walked through the hallways of Acedia. They looked all looked too familiar to Tom. He saw people standing around talking and enjoying life as they walked. It wasn't anything unusual and nothing to take Tom's concentration from talking with Clive.

"It's a place you haven't been before," Clive said with his back turned to Tom as they walked. This was an especially troubling answer to Tom who was hoping for something more concrete.

"What do you mean?" Tom asked. Clive turned a corner. It was a hallway Tom had never seen. But this wasn't something to note either since Tom hadn't been down many hallways in Acedia. Although this hallway was a little stranger than the others as it seemed to change color halfway through. On the side with Clive and Tom there were the normal florescent lights shining down on them illuminating where they were. As you looked to the other side of the hallway, the florescent light shifted gradually into a red tint. The lights still beat down heavily, but instead everything was almost painted with a red filter. This was particularly strange to Tom. Fear entered his body as the place across the hallway looked like a place he did not wish to go.

"Is that? Is that the entrance to the third floor?" Tom asked stuttering slightly. Clive turned around to look at him.

"No, it's the entrance to Phestiles," Clive said. Tom had heard the name before but never asked much about it. He knew he lived in Acedia but not much else about the rest of the Community Center.

"You've only ever known Acedia, a division of the Community Center where we find happiness and peace through endurance and perseverance. Phestiles is different...," Clive said turning his head back to the red light ahead. The ominous feeling was palpable to both men. Something felt wrong in this place and Tom wanted to find out why. Clive started stepping closer to the other end of the hall. Tom followed. On the far end where the hall split into two different hallways the men saw someone walk across. A citizen of Phestiles beating their closed fist against the wall as they walked. The person hung their head low and fist clinched in anger. They didn't take notice to Tom or Clive as they walked, but then again, the two men were not in Phestiles yet.

"Where do the people of Phestiles find peace?" Tom asked stepping forward with Clive.

"I don't think they truly look for happiness or peace. Anger, fear, and apathy are the only things they want from existence," Clive said as he started to inch closer to the wall next to them. Tom followed with him. The red from the other end of the hallway inched closer as they walked.

"Why would anyone want anger and fear?" Tom asked quietly.

"That's the thing. Most people do want anger and fear throughout existence at least once or twice. You, your parents, even Kate have probably been citizens of Phestiles," Clive said. His voice lowered as he inched forward. "Not to mention, but you've been with one of its citizens for the duration of your existence," Clive stopped to look at Tom.

"You're from Phestiles?" Tom asked. Clive expected some sort of surprise. Instead Tom was only curious.

"Yes. It's... not something I'm proud of and plan on moving back to Acedia eventually. I know it's because I haven't realized I don't want to exist this way. But other citizens and I are stuck in our own perfect world of fear and anger," Clive finished as he stopped just before the red touched his feet. He turned to look at Tom.

"Listen to me, keep your head down and follow me directly. Phestiles is not like Acedia where our division is decided electorally. Phestiles has a king who often lacks any sort of empathy for wanderers. He wishes to keep citizens like me for himself," Clive said staring at

Tom who listened carefully.

He turned back around and stepped into the red. Tom followed after but did not feel any different as they ventured. Sure, he saw things differently because of the red filter, but he did not feel much different than when he did in Acedia. The two men turned to the right. Here Tom saw a fairly normal looking hallway like he would see in Acedia. It was covered in red and the people... the people were different. Many of them were huddled together but some were screaming at each other in fights. Some sat on the ground with a bowl of food eating a brown mush. It wasn't a pleasant sight at all. All along the wall were large posters of a very serious man with a short beard. As they passed by Tom noticed a crown sitting on the man's head.

"It was a crown he believed was constructed by his closest confidants...," Clive whispered as they walked slowly. He knew Tom was curious about the king and why he stared with gloom at them all. "...People of his closest confidence he assumed gifted him this crown as a means to rule over Phestiles. Unlike most crowns in stories, its power came only from the weight it gave to whoever wore it," Clive continued as Tom listened carefully. He followed Clive closely looking at each poster as they walked through long corridors. Clive only spoke when very few people were in any given hallway.

"It's self-given by any citizen who wears it, but the citizens here dare not question the King of its ownership. The King, a citizen of the Community Center deeply wrought with fear and confusion sat only on a throne of greed and loneliness in a room separated by his own division."

The intense description of this King sent nothing but fear down Tom's own back. Long corridors followed by sharp turns kept Tom on his feet as he followed Clive. He moved slowly but with purpose along the walls of the smooth stone and would occasionally look down at a small journal he carried. It was the only remnant of when he first visited the third floor.

"The Kings advisors idly stand by. Some from Acedia and some I've heard are from a place no person has been. These advisors push him back and forth making decisions on behalf of his people who ultimately suffer the cost of never knowing a true king," Clive continued as they walked.

"It sounds awful in Phestiles," Tom whispered.

"Well, he is a rational king nonetheless," Clive said. Tom didn't understand how someone so lost in fear and hatred could ever be rational. "Understanding the Community Center is his strength in keeping division alive and growing. There's no room for mistakes here. His colorless throne is built only for himself and in knowing one day he too will walk through the curtain in an attempt to understand existence," Clive concluded his understanding of Phestiles and their King as he stopped at a large wooden door. The door was nothing special and something Tom thought they should have easily passed. It wasn't hidden by anything and it was easily accessible.

"This is it?" Tom asked puzzled.

"People think the path to evil is well lit and obvious. They believe it's something hidden in the darkest depths of even anger and hatred," Clive said as he walked in front of the door now standing up straight. "They think it would have a confusing riddle to reach involving complex puzzles with deadly consequences," Clive continued. "But that is not what I found. Evil is always much easier to find than one expects," Clive concluded as he grasped the handle and opened the door.

The two men looked inside. Just in front of them were an incredibly small set of concrete steps leading up. The steps were dark with few lights illuminating them. Tom was surprised at how close it was to the streets where anyone could stumble upon it. The door was not guarded by anyone the King may have placed there. The door was open to anyone. Clive turned to Tom before they entered.

"There's something you need to know before we go up. Evil may represent something but its form changes with every soul. For me, it was a dragon who sat at a desk ready to debate. The dragon was an illusion to Lucifer since I am a Christian. I don't know how evil will appear to you. Nor do I know exactly what will happen when you step onto the third floor," Clive said. Tom nodded. "Whatever you face will ask you to describe what you think it is. If you are right then you'll be given the chance to argue why you think it shouldn't be allowed to exist," Clive continued.

"I know the game. I was told about it," Tom said

abruptly and almost ready to run in.

"This isn't something trivial Tom. I know you. I think you have a different perspective to make real change. Understood?" Clive said before they walked up the steps.

Tom thought on this for a moment. If he were only doing this for Clive then it would be enough to probably turn him away. But Tom's curiosity and his need to find good for his wife triumphed over any attempt Tom had to leave. He nodded his head in agreement and the two men stepped inside.

"Why don't people use this more often?" Tom asked as they stepped up the winding stairs.

"They would if it were strange or a puzzle like entrance but it's just a door. There's no reason to investigate if it's only a door," Clive answered.

"People don't accidently open it and use the stairs finding evil?" Tom asked.

"They do all the time. Accidental or not, it's still evil," Clive answered cryptically. Tom understood his reason to find good in evil. However Tom didn't understand why he was on these steps about to argue with evil. He didn't understand Clive's reasoning behind it.

"What do you believe now?" Tom asked as they walked. Clive didn't turn around. He heard the question but only thought on it with every step they took. He remembered a time when he took this journey alone. He knew when he met Tom and who he was, but something shifted in him as he got to know Tom.

"Tom... do you know why I was at the curtain the

day I met you?" Clive asked continuing up the stairs. Tom thought for a moment but only remembered the crazed old man with the puzzle pieces.

"I think I remember you saying you thought on the curtain a lot also. That I reminded you of yourself," Tom replied innocently.

"Yes, you're right. But it's not the reason why I went to the curtain that day," he said as he stopped. He turned and looked down at Tom who stood only a few steps behind him.

"I was there to kill myself, Tom," Clive said with a deep breath and warrying tongue. Tom didn't know what to say or how to react to this. "I was questioning everything I knew because I met evil and I wasn't able to win...," Clive said as his eyes lowered to stare at the concrete. "...Where was god? Where was he on the third floor?" Clive asked as he raised his eyes to meet Tom's. Tom saw the same tears he saw in Kate's eyes appear in Clive's. "The answer? Nowhere. I couldn't see him. I couldn't see the good in evil. It was all darkness and evil. But you? There's something about you I knew I had to understand," Clive continued telling him. He took a moment and thought about his next words carefully. "In the time I've known you you've been nothing but selfish. You, you, you. It's always about you," Clive said. Tom felt a little hurt by this accusation but knew it were true in the end. "I thought to myself there is definitely something wrong with you. But you learned from that. I can see that now. So I know your selfishness wasn't what I was trying to understand. You know what was? Why I think you'll be able to defeat evil and see the good that I missed? Why your wife loves you? Why your father knew you could make it on the second floor?" Clive asked more passionately as Tom stood on the stairs.

He didn't know why any of these things happened. Whatever Clive said he knew was probably too much to say on his behalf. "Tom, it's because you're a child," he said breaking into a laugh. Tom smiled slightly because it almost sounded like an insult. "You question things without remorse Tom. You question God's world not because you're trying to prove a point but because you want to know. And you were selfish and horrible because... well... children are selfish and horrible...," he continued to laugh as Tom joined. "And I'm so glad when you learned more about the difference between what you want and what you can do for others... you didn't lose your questioning also. You didn't lose yourself as a child as you grew up," Clive said putting his hand on Tom's shoulder. "If anyone is going to see the good and defeat the evil... it's you Tom. Not because you're all powerful or even because you come from a place of weakness. But because you're only a child who's wandering through a forest seeking an answer," Clive concluded to tell Tom who was no less teary eyed by the speech.

Clive patted his shoulder and the two continued upward. Tom didn't think of himself as a child really. But maybe someone who questions is someone who could help others somehow... someway.

The two men stopped and stepped to the side revealing a white door with a silver handle. Tom knew this was the place as he stepped up to stand next to Clive.

"Any advice?" Tom asked. Clive smiled.

"Not for you... No. Everything will change from here on out," Clive said. Tom was quickly reminded of what Eric told him just before he left. Tom remembered on the first floor... time works differently. With this, Tom grasped the handle of the door and walked inside.

Chapter XXIII

The Most Powerful Being

Darkness filled his vision, but it only stayed as long as Tom remained still and silent. Something Tom was not. As he pushed himself forward the dark dissipated as it often does but transformed into what he saw before him. He saw light. In the light he saw something he did not quite expect to find. He didn't understand what he saw but what he did expect was something much worse. Of course, as anyone who goes to meet a great evil, Tom expected a large dragon or a demon like beast to greet him with fire and brimstone. Instead there were florescent lights shining down on him as he stepped onto blue well-kept carpet.

A woman sat behind a front-desk only feet in front of him. She looked king with deceit hiding behind her large eyes. Behind her, Tom saw a large sign in beautiful font reading "You Are". As Tom walked closer to the counter where the woman sat he saw underneath the sign it contained a caption reading "May you be safe. May you be healthy. May you be happy. May you live with ease." It was a kind and warm welcome to read. Something Tom didn't expect to see in the place known as evil.

The woman at the desk smiled at him excitedly. Tom couldn't help but smile back at how comfortably excited she was to greet him. It was as if Tom was always expected to show up and she waited patiently only for him. Tom thought about what this could mean. He wondered why this place felt so warm and welcoming. He asked himself questions in innocent ignorance as children do.

"Hi!" the young woman said as if bubbles exuded from her.

"Why are you so happy and excited?" Tom immediately asked her matching the enthusiasm. This question wasn't something she necessarily expected as most only accepted the joy they were given when they walked in. Her smile didn't disappear but she tilted her head slightly. Tom thought for a moment she was actually thinking about the question before she suddenly changed the subject.

"Do you have an appointment?" she asked looking down at a sheet of paper on the desk. Tom scratched the back of his head and looked behind him, then back at her.

"No, did I need one?" he asked her politely.

"No! That was a joke!" she said laughing hysterically. She came around to the other side of the desk. Tom gave her a small chuckle to mask the fact that he didn't understand her joke.

"You are very happy. Why is that?" Tom asked again pressing her to answer his question. Again, she didn't change her smile but tilted her head to try and think of an answer. Tom felt uncomfortable as he watched the gears turn inside her head.

"You will be able to answer all your questions," her eyes stared into Tom with her head still slightly tilted as she made the strange comment.

"Me? But I'm the one asking the question?" Tom asked puzzled.

"Exactly. You ask the question. You have the answer," she replied turning around to open a plain white door and golden handle. It opened into a hallway where the blue carpet continued. As they walked through there were many openings with other people sitting in small cubicles. Occasionally one would look at the two of them with a big smile on their face. Tom noticed these strange people and was just about to ask the young woman about who they were when he saw another person walking opposite of them. He wore a white shirt and dark red tie. He looked... normal. He looked happy and healthy. Every person Tom saw looked... normal. This man nodded to the young woman as they walked and spoke to Tom freely.

"Best decision you'll ever make," he whispered passing by. Tom felt the man pat him on the back which sent a shiver down his spine. Tom was feeling discomfort in a place that only wanted to make him feel comfortable. As if a veil of lies was draped over him so he would believe some theatrical show they were putting on for him.

Eventually the woman came to a door at the end of the very long hallway and opened it without hesitation. It's important to note this because Tom felt as though every nook and cranny in this place was open to him at all times. As though he could actually stop following the woman and she would be fine with it. As if he could go and speak with any of the other people and everyone would be happy to join him in conversation. Something Tom noticed about this feeling was the lack of thinking about the door he came through. Tom only thought about the place he was in and had no thought about anything on the first floor or the second floor. He knew he was in the Community Center. He knew he was on the third floor. But Tom's entire focus was on the place he was in. It was as if he couldn't think about anything other than exploring the third floor and almost felt as if the third floor was the only floor to exist at all.

"Why can't I think about anything other than where I am?" Tom asked the woman just before she grasped the handle to another plain door. She turned around and smiled at him caringly.

"You can Tom. You can do anything you want here," she told him confidently. Tom was not amused.

"No, I can't. I keep trying to think about the first floor or even the second floor, but I can't. I had friends there. I had family and an existence there," he told her almost frantically now. She, again, tilted her head and again, Tom could see the gears in her head slowly turning.

"Maybe because the only *real* you is on the third floor with us," she said after a moment of silence. She quickly turned around and grabbed the handle again.

"Are you saying I only exist on the third floor?" he asked her just before she could open it. She turned around again with the usual smile.

"You will have the answer," she said. This time she turned around and swung the door open just before Tom could ask her any more questions.

Through the door was nothing tremendously special, although she acted as if it was. Tom heard her gasp in delight as she ran inside. Following behind her, Tom stepped inside where the blue carpet ended and a hard wood floor began. Looking around the average room Tom saw it was a circular shape. The walls were an off-white color and the same fluorescent lights beat down on him in the hallway shown bright in this room. The young woman ran behind a desk at the far end of the room giving a hug to... something.

Tom wanted to say it was a man, but it didn't quite resemble a man. The young woman quickly left after giving this *thing* a hug and walked back outside closing the door. This left Tom looking around at the room with this strange thing sitting at a desk staring at him. The "man" wore the same shirt and tie the others outside wore but with the additional suit jacket draped over him. His face was incredibly handsome, and his teeth shown beautifully white. Dark hair on his head was freshly cut to only frame a more handsome face. Tom didn't stare long. Instead he continued to walk to where the desk was and sat down. The man kept smiling until he opened his mouth to speak, only to be cut off by Tom.

"I assume you're '*you*'?" Tom asked as his eyes still looked around the room. The man's eyes contorted slightly at Tom's statement. "That's what this is right? I come to the third floor. I can't think of the first or second floor. The woman at the front tells me only I have the answers but in a weird cryptic way where she says the word '*you*'," Tom explained to the man who slowly closed his mouth allowing Tom to continue speaking. "Basically I'm supposed to come to some realization that *I* am the evil in the Community Center, right? Looking at *you* is really looking at *me* yada yada yada," Tom stopped speaking and looked back at the man who now had a grin on his odd-looking face.

"Look at the man who's figured it out. Bravo," he spoke with perfect diction and absolute authority of the third floor.

"It's not hard to figure out," Tom said as his eyes floated back to the man who looked as though he was breaking character.

"So, you already know who I am? There is no need for the game?" he said casually.

"That's the real problem," Tom said taking a moment to think. The man across the desk did not break his smile but in his eyes Tom saw his character shine through. Tom looked at them and saw a man trying to figure out where the next pieces would move. Pieces on a chess board primed for a winner and loser. Tom didn't care much for chess. Tom was partial to puzzles though. Tom only cared about the answers.

"What is the problem?" he asked.

"I don't know what you are," Tom said admittedly. "It's obvious what you're doing here with the thin veil. You're trying to convince whoever is here *they* are the embodiment of evil. But seeing your veil doesn't explain why I can't think of anything outside of the third floor. It doesn't explain what you are because even if you hold up a mirror to me and say *you* are *me* and I am *you*. It doesn't answer the next question, who am *I*?" Tom explained to the façade of a man. He leaned back in his chair; his lips closed together hiding his shining teeth, but his smile remained. He looked up at the ceiling thinking of an answer. The previous person who came to him was as simple at guessing what he was and debating. Tom was more interested in the structure of the argument rather than the argument itself.

"Who are you? Who am I?" the man asked repeating what Tom explained. It was an important question. Tom is saying in no uncertain terms that if anyone (including the literal being of evil) claims they are *you*, it begs the question, who are you? The game evil wanted to play was not only a question of what evil *is*, but of who Tom *was*.

"You are everything the first and second floor need, Tom. You are what the Community Center needs. You are what the world needs," the man said still staring at the ceiling.

"If you are me then that's myself telling me what I am...," Tom said continuing his thoughts. "Maybe it is true. Maybe I am god. Maybe... I am everything," Tom finished his thought. He remembered back to when he had the same idea on the second floor only to be cut off by the Captain. But now, he was with a being allowing him to explore this thought.

The man sitting at the desk not only allowed Tom to explore these thoughts but encouraged it. Tom had an absolute freedom to go as far with his thoughts as he wanted. The man wanted Tom to find his answer and stop questioning. The man wanted Tom to find the puzzle piece and be content. Tom wanted to continue even further after finding his answer.

"After all, no one can prove they're even conscious right?" the man said looking back to Tom, mimicking arguments he'd had on the first floor.

"Exactly, I can't know anyone around me is even conscious in the same way I am. My thought processes are my own. My dreams and life are my own and no other person can compare or even prove they experience anything the same way I do," Tom said almost forgetting about the man who sat in front of him. Tom simply kept moving forward with the discussion. A place the man greatly wanted him to remain.

"It only stands to reason; you are the only one conscious. You are god," the man said, his lips separating to reveal his strange smile. It seemed this is the answer the man wanted Tom to find and be complacent in. But Tom did not find answers only to stop his questions. He did not want an answer only to check the boxes of a question, he wanted *the* answer.

"If those around me can't prove they're conscious. How can I expect to prove my own consciousness to any of them?" Tom asked himself.

The smile disappeared from the man's face. Tom was starting to ask questions beyond the answer he was given. No matter how uneducated or ridiculous the questions sounded, Tom was simply shooting into the dark to see if there was anything else he could find. Tom didn't know, but he did find something else. He may just not know it currently but what he said next forced the man to actually change his tune about the entire conversation. The man slowly realized he was not speaking with an educated philosopher, theologian, or even a man with answers. The man was speaking with a child.

"...I can't prove my consciousness to them... and by that notion... you?" Tom asked as his eyes met with the man. It was as if Tom suddenly remembered they were having a conversation.

"I know you're conscious because I *am* you," the man said almost with defense in his voice. Tom took no notice. Tom was not a man on the offense but a man who only wanted to continue seeking an answer.

"Exactly...," Tom said surprising the man. "...if you

are *me* then I should know you are conscious. But I don't. And now I can ask the question, who are *you*?" Tom explained. The man tried to think of an answer but only silence filled the space between them. Simple tricks and manipulation to have Tom believe he was the top of the Community Center were not working. "You're not me...," Tom said looking away from the man again and attempting to piece it together. "...and if you're not me then you're not any of them out there like you've deceitfully shown," Tom said gesturing to the door behind referencing the men and women in the office behind him.

"You're of course right. You are very discerning," the man said hoping to halt any further investigation by Tom.

"Maybe you are god. Maybe god is evil," Tom said with wide eyes looking at the desk instead of the man. He questioned the scenario he was in as if he were an outsider and not someone experiencing it currently.

"An equally right answer. You've done it. I am god. If I'm not then I would be just like any other person on the first or second floor. It's clear I have power over all things in the Community Center. So, I must be god," the man said setting the palms of his hands on the desk as if he were about to stand up.

"Which god?" Tom asked crossing his arms and leaning back in his chair. The man leaned back in his chair slightly annoyed.

"You're a Christian. You tell me," he asked. Tom was a Christian according to his ballot. Did Tom mean the Christian god or was there another god he didn't know much about? He repeated the word "god" in his mind over and over again curious to its meaning.

"I think I misunderstand what god means...," he said under his breath. "...all powerful doesn't mean most powerful...," Tom continued whispering to himself. "...all powerful means from the least to the most. All-encompassing power," Tom said.

"And? What are you getting at?" the man's voice was clearly filled with an annoyance which was lost to Tom.

"Same with all knowing. It means knowing the least and knowing everything equally. From the few to the many... the least to the most... from life...," Tom paused as the curtain flashed before his eyes. "...to death...," he said trying to think about the curtain more than the flash but couldn't bring himself to think of any person on the first floor or what his story even was. Tom only continued attempting to understand. His eyes shot back to the man who watched Tom's excavation. "...but you. You're the most powerful in the Community Center and in Earth. You're the most knowing. You're the most everything. You are the top," Tom said sounding as if he were in reverence of evil.

"I'm flattered," the man said.

"Don't be...," Tom shot back. "...because it means you're not all powerful. It means you're not god," Tom said.

"But like you asked. Which god?" the man asked thinking for a moment he cornered Tom.

"It's not 'which god'. It is only God. And you're not him," Tom said after a moment of silence trying to figure out which god was the right one on his ballot.

"But it *is* still 'which god'...," the man said almost not believing Tom would simply ignore this question. "... There's a multitude of them on the precious ballot everyone carries. The one in your pocket right now. One of those gods has to be the right one. One of them has to be god," the man said with his smile slowly starting to form again.

"Then the God who doesn't exist," Tom said with a sudden breath and almost sigh of relief.

"How can that be? A god who doesn't exist?" the man asked quizzically. And Tom thought again for a moment about what he meant.

"Because if any god exists, then it is on the same plane of existence as you or I. It exists as any person on Earth or in the Community Center...," Tom said as if the words were as easy to pick as flowers in a fully grown garden. "...I could have the same conversation with any god that exists about being most powerful. Every person wants their god to be on top of the Community Center. Every person wants the third floor to be for them. When we discover only evil on the third floor then people assume this is what god is. This must be. We think because evil is everywhere that we are the ones to either change it or embrace it. The mistake is in thinking god is on top of the world. God is both. He is with the least and he is with the most. He doesn't exist because he *is* existence," Tom said trying to think every word through.

"Then it begs the question of course...," the man said as if he were the only one playing a game of chess still. "...where is this god who *is* existence? Who is this being who is beyond the ballot? This being you claim is with us even here and now?" the man asked hoping to push Tom again into a corner.

"I don't know," Tom said immediately. The man chuckled at his answer.

"Look at you, as if you have any clue as to what you speak. You are certainly a child walking through a theological garden plucking at low hanging fruit," the man said mocking Tom.

"There is something here with you and I," Tom said, his eyes now wide again. "If you weren't in this room... I wouldn't be alone," Tom said looking at the man. Instead of only engaging in conversation, Tom picked up a pencil from the desk in front of him. "If you weren't in this room, I could look at this pencil and know I'm not alone. Why? Because this pencil exists, just as I do," Tom said placing the pencil back on the desk. With this knowledge, Tom stood up from his chair. The man followed him with his eyes. "As much as I'd like to tell you what you are and debate you until I banish you from all of existence. It's simply not my place. You're on this side of the curtain just as I am. You exist just like me and this pencil. You are on this scale of goodness and evil just like every other person. I don't care for you or what you do. There's nothing I can do about the horrible atrocities you commit in the name of evil on the first and second floor. I cannot banish you. The only thing I can do? Is overcome you," Tom said turning around to the door he entered. The man stood from his desk suddenly in furious anger.

"I am the top of the Community Center! I am everything you want to be and more! I am you and you are me!" the man screamed as Tom grasped the door handle, opened it, and exited the room. Tom knew the man claimed to be the top of the Community Center just as evil claims to be the most powerful on Earth. But what Tom sought was not the most powerful. What Tom sought after was a God who didn't exist.

Chapter XXIV

Nods and Sighs

Tom didn't feel normal when he left the third floor. Walking through the door back into darkness he knew there would be a light just as he'd entered. He expected to see the same thing he saw when he found its entrance. He assumed there would be the winding staircase he would walk down and find the door to the gloomy Phestiles. This would make too much sense for things to unfold nice and neat in the Community Center. Instead, the darkness flooded his field of vision. He started to feel something in his body rather than anything external. He tried to look down at his hands, but they were still painted with darkness just like the rest of his vision. As light started to fade in, so did his hands. To his surprise they were covered in wrinkles and skin loosely fitting around his bones. This didn't take Tom completely off guard because accompanied with the sudden change in his appearance were memories of the Community Center he never knew he had. He looked up from his hands and as the light formed in front of him he heard a loud door shut from behind. Turning around Tom saw a church he'd just exited, not the entrance to the third floor. He recognized the church as one he visited long ago in his youth. It was a place he came to when things felt confusing and he hoped to find answers. Regardless of the debate over truth, churches were often referred to as a place where one could find answers.

Turning around Tom saw the wide-open concrete space stopped by various shops and houses. He now remembered he'd never actually exited the church in his youth either. The story of meeting the man and woman in the church came back to him. He felt a sudden anxious fear of leaving the church because of protestors outside resenting him. But now, Tom exited.

Sitting in the open space were a group of elderly people holding signs. The signs relaxed against the peoples shoulders as well as on the ground lying flat. It was clear to Tom the small group of people were tired and ready to give up their cause. Tom thought it almost admirable they'd been protesting for such a long time for whatever cause they believed in. By the same coin he didn't understand exactly why they would protest for so long. If he were a younger man in earlier chapters, he probably would have ignored the group of people as he did with the angry people fighting over a painting of a bear and rabbit. But these people were no longer fighting. Both Tom and these people had aged beyond their years.

He walked calmly to one of the men sitting down who had a sign leaning against his shoulder reading "God is a bigot". Tom didn't care much for the sign and didn't want to get into a theological discussion with the man over which god or what actions god took making him a bigot. The sign clearly was something the man firmly believed. No one would protest it for so long if it weren't something they truly believed.

"You've been here for a long time," Tom said as he bent down to sit next to the man. The man slowly lifted his eyes. As they came into Tom's view he could see just how horribly tired the man was. The man grasped with everything he had to hold on to his existence.

"I can't rest until evil is purged from the Community Center. I can't rest until evil is purged from our books," the old man said with a crackling voice just barely able to form words. His eyes were glossy and almost blind as they looked away from Tom

"Evil," Tom sighed and said the word out loud to himself. The man had no idea, but Tom had just encountered what most considered the embodiment and reflection of what evil was. He also didn't know Tom felt pretty good about his encounter with the man on the third floor.

"Us!" the man suddenly said. It was as if the man yelled but didn't have enough energy to raise his voice much higher than Tom's voice. "We are the evil... we are the dreaded cancer," the man said. Tom could sense the resentment the man had toward existence.

"The self. Including you?" Tom asked confidently.

"Of course. I am evil. I am of an oppressive group only trying to unlearn my inherent privileges," he said to Tom.

"I don't know," he said engaging with the man's conversation.

Tom thought about the times Clive told him about the attempts people made against the embodiment of evil and all failing one after the other. He thought about this man spending his entire life hoping to rid evil with protests and screams of injustice. "It seems people are so obsessed with destroying evil that they forget to ever walk into goodness," Tom said looking at the church in front of them.

"We can't move forward until evil is destroyed," the man said with a small chuckle of laughter in his voice. Tom was an old man as well but not nearly as old as this man. He could feel the elderly man looking down on him as if Tom had no idea what he talked about. Which, to be frank, is justified.

"I don't think I agree with you...," Tom said. He noticed out of the corner of his eye the man's hand gripped his sign just a little tighter. As if Tom's disagreement was a form of violence and conflict he had to prepare for. But Tom persisted. "...The answer to evil is not evil," Tom concluded his thought.

"Sometimes you must fight fire with fire," the man said. Tom saw the man's jawline contort slightly showing he was growing tense. He was no longer the tired old man but sparked a fight as soon as Tom disagreed.

"That's a term coined on the second floor meant to put out fires. Firefighters would burn patches, so the uncontrolled fire didn't have anywhere to go. It's not the same thing," Tom added.

"Then what do you suggest? Just let evil be where it is? Let the atrocities of the world exist?" the man asked throwing one of his hands in the air in defiance.

"Pointing a finger at me and grouping me with evil won't help the case to destroy evil either...," Tom said immediately. Tom was starting to enjoy his older age. He had a little bit more backbone but also had the same thought process he did when he was younger. "Pointing a finger at this church or anyone inside does no good either...," Tom said gesturing to the large wooden doors of the church. "But don't mistake my unwillingness to point fingers as somehow bending the knee," Tom said.

"I only point to those who need to leave," the man said looking away.

"You point to those who exist just as you," Tom continued. "The answer to evil isn't evil. The answer to evil is goodness," Tom emphasized.

"So you're one of those people who thinks everything should be sunshine and roses," the elderly man scoffed surprising Tom.

"You misunderstand what goodness is," Tom replied.

"Enlighten me. How do I shake hands with the racist?" the man asked.

"You don't...," Tom said starting to think heavier on the question.

After all, how does one shake hands with those who bend the knee to evil? How does someone shake hands with people who side on everything that's wrong with this world? Tom didn't like thinking about this question. One of the only questions he didn't enjoy exploring. Because at the foundation of the Community Center and every book on the second floor, evil existed. Evil was not some man in a tailored suit to have a philosophical conversation with. No, evil was horrible. Most think they've seen evil because they've witnessed atrocities on the news or heard about it from a friend of a friend. Rarely has a person actually seen it. I'm thankful to say the author of this book has not seen evil and can only describe the absence of what he has seen, which is goodness.

How can one shake hands with an evil most don't even know? The sort of evil that men find power in and evil men use to corrupt entire groups. Tom was not one to shy away from the question as he looked back at the old man's glossy and fading eyes. Something the man said on the third floor was rooted in a truth. Evil does reside in everyone. In Tom, evil rested. In this old man, evil rested.

"How can you hold hands with anyone at all if you can't with yourself?" Tom asked suddenly.

"How do you mean?" the man asked.

"You've sat in front of this church your entire existence. You've boiled in angry protest every day. You've past by any form of discipline on your own existence...," Tom said staring at the church still letting the words flow out. "...you have no existence," Tom whispered but loud enough to be heard. "How can you expect to overcome evil when you can't overcome your own?" Tom said looking back at the man who was paying close attention.

"I'm not as evil as those in there," the man stood on his defense headstrong. "I chose my existence and those inside the church chose theirs," the man exclaimed with self-given righteous anger.

"You're right," Tom said silently.

He realized there was no arguing with the man. They were no longer discussing but were now debating. Here Tom made an interesting discovery as to what he thought 'evil' could be. Tom knew he was wrong, about pretty much everything in his entire life. He didn't know anything. He certainly didn't know what was after the curtain. And any belief he checked off he would know to be wrong. This man sitting next to him, was *right*. How can that be? Tom looked around at the group sitting with their signs. Every person in the group was right. He looked back to the church. Every person inside the church was right. He thought about every person he'd come across in his time in the Community Center and how every person he'd met was *right*.

"The greatest lie evil ever told was convincing everyone it didn't exist," the man said under his breath.

This didn't make any sense either. Tom met evil and at no point did it seem any bit interested to convince him it didn't exist. Why would evil care if people knew if it existed or not? It didn't matter. People would choose to do evil with or without labelling it as such.

"The greatest lie evil ever told was convincing everyone they are *right*," Tom said as he started to stand. The man didn't say anything to Tom and only continued to stare at the church. The man would always be right. He would be right in his protest, no matter the cost. Tom walked away no closer to understanding existence or the curtain.

Chapter XXV

The Years to Come

It's been a while since we've spoken. Although present in every chapter I sometimes don't speak and only let the story and characters play out the way they do. The author knows this because he gets tied up in the story forgetting about me. That's quite alright, I don't mind. Several people have already said I'm not the easiest part of the book to read but I digress.

You're almost through the authors second book. That's exciting. At the same time what is the story building towards? There isn't any way the author can actually describe what's beyond the curtain in any way that would satisfy Tom's need to know more. So let's recap the events of the book simply and see where things have gotten us.

Tom was an old man now. He'd read his own book

and knew how his existence would conclude. He knew the curtain was only a simple stroll away for him. Let's look at his life or at least this small existence of his. He arrived at the Community Center and immediately wanted to know what was after the curtain. Existence was finite for him and he didn't care to live in the moment when the curtain could change everything about whatever existence held. Tom concluded pretty quickly he didn't know what was after the curtain. There was no belief on the ballot he thought could be any more knowing than any other belief. After all, everything in existence was on Tom's side of the curtain.

He met a strange man with a puzzle piece who obsessed over questioning and would hand out puzzle pieces to the citizens. Tom didn't want to be like all the other people grasping firmly onto puzzle pieces as if they knew their piece would somehow fit. So standing in front of Clive and the man, he placed his on the ground. Now he was free to question as much as he wanted without the weight of any current belief about the missing puzzle piece.

It was here when Tom met his own mother and she only confused him further. The idea of the puzzle piece left his mind, and he was faced with understanding the actual working of existence. He learned more about the different divisions of the Community Center. This, for you, hopefully hinted at a slightly larger universe the author could possibly return to in future books. Tom learned time on the first floor moved fluidly, and events unfolded out of sync from people's perceptions.

The first floor was where everything is jumbled and moved around. Even now the effects of the first floor are apparent.

For example, Eric hasn't shown up to the Community Center yet even after a lifelong friendship with Tom. Kate, his wife, had passed behind the curtain long ago even though it wasn't physically that long ago when Tom saw them both as his son's funeral. His mother told him of the second floor where he might find more answers to what's after the curtain. It was where time ran linear.

So, Tom continued his search and found himself on the second floor where he learned what a book was. He found out what happened to David, his son, and a new belief was introduced to him by the Captain of the second floor. It was still just a belief like every other belief on the ballot. There was still something missing for Tom. He was missing the answer. Tom was missing what *was* and not just a *belief.* He didn't want to only believe in something but wanted to know it to be true.

When Tom came back to the first floor from the second he attended David's memorial where a good friend of his explained Tom needed to meet evil. Tom was fairly hesitant. But this friend did show him the way to the second floor and his wife couldn't bear to understand why David died. She couldn't see the good in any of this madness and so Tom had to at least attempt to find it for her. There had to be good. Tom unfortunately returned from the third-floor empty handed. He found no good on the third floor but instead spoke to a man with an awkward smile. But what was goodness? Tom often asked himself the question especially since he barely knew what evil was. At least he knew evil did exist, but he didn't much care for it. He didn't really have any opinion about what the root of all evil was. To him, it didn't matter. What mattered was finding the good. Why? Because if "something is" then it is inherently something. That is an attribute of the "something". Which means it is not *nothing*. And if it is something then it's positive to a negative. Negative being the evil, and positive being the good.

Tom only searched out the good. He needed to know there was good. As Tom came down from the third floor it was very important for him to remember Eric's last words to him about remembering how time worked differently on the first floor. All of his family and friends were long gone. Tom was alone in the Community Center now. Tom was in his later years. He was almost ready to go beyond the curtain and he knew it. He also knew he still didn't know what he believed.

Tom looked down at his ballot as he sat in a chair. The chair was at the first table where him and Eric had their first conversation. It was near the chicken restaurant and people bustled around just as they always did. He thought of the woman who told him to experience the chicken tenders as if they were the only thing he would experience. He thought about Eric mocking the woman and then basically telling him the same thing but through an atheistic point of view.

The ballot remained sitting in front of Tom with no

answer he could find. There were so many different choices. He didn't know if it mattered even if he did mark something. Maybe he should just throw it away like some people. Was this moment about him? Was this moment about existence in general? He concluded earlier several times through his story that existence actually wasn't about him at all. Sometimes existence was about his wife. Sometimes existence was about his son. What could his existence be about if not for himself? Was it only for others as he previously thought? He wanted so desperately to have more answers than when he was younger, but he found himself in the same place he was all those years ago and the years to come.

"And the years to come," Tom whispered to himself sitting alone. He thought heavily on those words for a moment. "And the years to come," meaning Tom would always have these thoughts and feelings. Would these questions change behind the curtain? Something would have to be so undeniably true for Tom not to question anything's existence. Just as he told the man on the third floor, how could he believe in any god that existed? If Tom walked behind the curtain and there stood a being with a great white beard and Tom stood with his regular physical body. How could he not question that being? Why is his beard white? Where do the wrinkles on his head come from? If he exists then who put him into existence just as every person has been placed into existence? The being, just as the man on the third floor, exists just like Tom does. In this narrative of existence Tom knew he was only still on the scale just like any other being from most powerful to least powerful.

This fact discouraged Tom unlike it excited him on the third floor. It discouraged him because, of course, he could be wrong just like every other time in his existence. Tom was wrong about everything so how could he not be wrong about what's after the curtain? Tom believed no one knew anything. Any belief on the ballot could be right. How could he be wrong about this belief also?

"Dad?"

The voice broke Tom's concentration and was all too familiar to him. It was the voice he recognized from the first moment he was on the bus and the voice he recognized from the book he read on the second floor. He looked up from where he sat and saw a familiar face. Tom's eyes watered. Standing next to the table in front of him stood David Lewis, his son. Tom stood from his chair quickly knocking it over embracing his son with a tight hug. Tom didn't care about anything else. He only cared about the embrace in the moment. It wasn't soon until Tom realized his son's arms were not around him. There was no return embrace from David.

Tom let go and stepped back to look at his son. David looked just as he did in the first chapter. Which didn't make any sense did it? But it did. When Tom arrived with his son at the Community Center he met David at the end of his journey. He'd never met David during his Community Center stay. There must have been moments like this they had spent together. Tom remembered what Eric told him again.

"Time works differently on the first floor."

Something was wrong. Something was strange. David stared at Tom without saying anything. Tears could be seen in David's eyes but were unable to run down his face. Tom grabbed him and hugged him again, but Tom still felt no embrace. David only stood in place allowing his father to try and embrace him as many times as he could. There were no changes. David couldn't or wouldn't embrace his father. It was as if David was still standing alone.

"Are you okay? David?" Tom asked his son who remained silent. Tom thought quickly about anything he could do. He felt his time in existence was coming to an end. Tom first met David at the end of his life, it made sense for David to meet Tom at the end of his own life. As much as Tom questioned his entire existence, he cared deeply about his son and wanted to let him know how sorry he was. He wanted to make it up to him. Tom knew he could show David something he would enjoy the rest of his life if he could show him anything at all.

Tom quickly ran to a side shop next to the chicken restaurant. Inside Tom grabbed a few ingredients and quickly made his way back to where David stood alone. David looked as though he were in a trance and unable to make heads or tails of existence. Tom placed the food on the table. Bread, honey ham, chips, and mustard, but his son remained silent. It wasn't anything

David knew yet. Tom quickly put the ingredients together.

"This is something you and your mother share together often and will bond over. Never lose that bond. I hope you understand how much she loves you," Tom said as he completed making the sandwich for David. His hands were shaking from nervousness, but also from understanding that he would no longer see his son after this moment. It was the only parting gift he could give him. Tom placed the sandwich in a bag and handed it to David who took the sandwich and looked at it. He didn't say anything.

"You will never know how much your mother and I care," Tom whispered. "But you're gone. And this version of you only sees me as the man who was never there," Tom said looking up at David. "I'm sorry David. I really am. I want to be there for you now more than ever," Tom said.

Again, David didn't say anything. Instead, he turned around with the sandwich in his hand and left. Tom knew even if he chased him, the David he saw would never see him. He was from the time when Tom completely abandoned him, and their timelines didn't cross.

Tom sat back down at the table. He reached into the bread bag and made himself another sandwich. He took a bite slowly and swallowed. This bite didn't feel normal. Tom looked at the Community Center where he first entered, and his eyesight started to jitter slightly. His vision contorted. Tom looked down at his sandwich and saw the outlines of his food start to emphasize. Each line connected with another objects outline until Tom saw it was all one large picture instead of individual pieces coming together.

Tom grinned. He knew something was happening and tried not to question any of it. Instead, Tom thought about his son and the sandwich in his hand. More lines appeared in front of Tom. The edge of the lines started to move slightly. Tom squinted to see what was happening and he saw lines start to vibrate and bounce even as people continued to move through the space in front of him. Tom looked at his hand closely. The lines forming his hand moved up and down like waves until he saw small letters begin to appear. Little letters formed all around his hand in odd structures not forming any words he knew. Putting his hand down he could see everything in the Community Center did the same. The letters bounced up and down in a dance he loved to watch.

Tom stood up from his chair, knowing it was his time. He walked towards the only place he knew he needed to go. He walked down the hallway filled with pictures of people who'd passed on. He stepped into the park where so many people still watched their loved ones go beyond the curtain. He continued walking towards the center where the large black curtain stood. Even on the curtain, letters bounced up and down almost calling him specifically to it. He didn't turn around but wondered if any of his family or friends came to watch him go.

This wasn't suicide. This was Tom's time to walk

through. He'd spent his time in the Community Center and in his book. It was time for him to go beyond whatever was held on the other side of the curtain. He touched the fabric and stopped for a moment before going beyond. One thing Tom would never change about himself was his need to question things. If a being with a flowing beard stood behind the curtain, so be it. But he would want to know everything about him. If he stepped behind the curtain and he swam in the river of fire forever to be burned in hell, he would want to know more about it. Tom only wanted to seek.

Tom grasped the curtains fabric, lifted it, and walked through. Thomas Lewis had died.

Chapter XXVI

Into the Unknown

Thomas Lewis died. His vision blurred from attempting to swallow a bite of the very sandwich I spoke about in the beginning of this book. The sandwich that simply *was*... having no connection to either good or evil. It was good to Tom and so it was. Just before Tom's death at an old age, he questioned his existence in the Community Center. Because... of course he did. He thought about the type of existence he was constantly seeking answers for and now that he was just about to go into the unknown, was no closer than when he stepped off the bus.

Yes, Tom learned many things but only within the narrative of the Community Center. And why should he give any credence to the Community Center? Even evil was a part of the Community Center. There was no way to know what truth was but only the path of belief in one's own puzzle piece or mark on a small ballot stuffed in their pocket. Tom's own religion of Christianity had many arguments for why it was the one true belief and could even still be the right belief. But then again... it was a belief. I repeat myself though, it was obvious Tom questioned existence and the reasons for being there, but never did he think (at least in the beginning) it would be something to waver the actions he took. That is, until he read his own book. Leading him where we are now.

I'm certain you're wondering where *here* is exactly. Where is this place called "now"? For the author it's as he writes the book. For you, the reader, it's whenever you're conveniently at this point in the book and reading these words. For Tom? Now that's something else entirely. It's the last chapter of the book. It's the chapter bringing it all together in a nice little bow for you to set the book down and say, "What an engaging story with a satisfying ending," the problem with this story is that it ends in death. Not in the sense that you've known death. Where your body shuts down and humans have no idea what happens. No, this story ends with Thomas Lewis walking behind the curtain.

What is it about the Community Center and its inhabitants that forces people to understand it is indeed time for them to walk behind the curtain? At what point are they going about their everyday lives and suddenly realize it's their time? Well, that's exactly what I'll be describing to you in just a moment. What did Tom see as he set his sandwich down on the plate forcing him to realize it was time for him to walk through the curtain without question? The reaction to one's death takes on many forms. Hopefully the story presented has led you to questioning even more about what is after death and exactly where Tom is currently.

You see, the author is given a difficult task of creating an intriguing and different idea for what is after death. Does Tom meet the Christian God and go directly to hell or somehow end up in heaven? Maybe Tom dies and nothing happens leaving the mystery wide open for the lifetimes of interpretation by everyday people. I already know where the author is going to take the story because if you've been paying awfully close attention, and I mean with the intention of attempting to understand where Tom will eventually go, the answer is made clear throughout the book. I'm not human. I'm not the author. I'm not the reader. I am the words on the page interwoven between every single aspect of the letters spread across the page.

Before I continue I must lay down some fundamentals of what you're about to read. So often when you read or watch a movie about the afterlife you see the person just as they were but now labeled "dead". As if whatever happens after death is just the dead version of yourself. If life were easy, then maybe the afterlife would be just so. But life is not easy, and existence in the Community Center even more confusing, and so the afterlife is going to be that much more confusing.

Let's talk about the concept of "feeling" for a moment. When you touch something, your brain reacts and knows it touched something. What this means is that *physically* you must be conscious so that you can feel. Without consciousness you cannot feel and without your body to react then you would suspect that there is no feeling at all. So, when I say Thomas Lewis is dead, what I am saying is he has no ability to feel because he no longer encompasses his body. His brain functionality has ceased completely. He walked behind the curtain and is no longer physically able to feel. The only reason we believe he could exist somewhere is because the alternative is something much darker, that Tom is nothing. This idea coincidently is a belief on the ballot, something Eric believed. Tom is simply gone. Maybe Tom walked behind the curtain and humanity made up some magical far away physical land where he's been transported to. It's either this or the alternative of nothingness.

We've already discussed the idea of nothingness haven't we? I hate nothingness. Because it's impossible. And if "nothing is impossible", then we can conclude one thing from Tom's journey. He is in some form or another still existing. This begs the immediate question, where is he? I know I've been teasing this ever since the start of the book but it's important to understand exactly what Tom is and where he is. And how... he... is. Or... when... Tom... is. Anyway, we've established he no longer has a body. It died and he has moved beyond the curtain. All these questions Tom's actually asking himself... even without a brain or body.

I promise we're getting to the point of where he is. I need you to understand phrases that I'll be using before we see where he is. When I say "Tom feels something" do not mistake it for him having a body. When one "feels" without a body it is not anything like what any person has experienced in existence. A good analogy is to think of the human body as a lens from which you feel things through. You touch something and your body is the middleman between you and whatever you felt. When you die, there is no more body. There is no more lens. There is no more filter to feel through. The only word to describe how a being "feels" after its body has deceased would be... pure. If Tom feels happy, his chest no longer beats faster. He doesn't smile. He doesn't laugh outrageously. It might sound a little sad at first, but you must distance yourself from what it means to *feel* happy. He doesn't do those things because those are just representations of what happiness is. Tom is feeling not a representation of happiness, he *is* pure happiness.

There is no way to beat around the bush now. We're about to see where Tom has gone after death and it... without mincing words... is very weird. Since you are reading this as a story, I must warn you that grammatically things are going to be very strange. What happens next is something that would blur the line between life and what happens after death. The author obviously can't show you what's after death because every person still exists and must finish their own book. But it is possible to maybe understand a perspective from the author that could be a glimpse behind the curtain. Afterall, the author of the book has had only one goal. It's not that he believes this is what actually happens after death. The goal of this book is to show you that whatever you think to be true, is only a belief in what you think to be true. What happens next only holds a mirror to the absolute depth of unknowing humanity has for anything we claim to understand. You want to know where Tom is? So does he.

"Where... where am I?" Tom asked himself. He could hear the mumble of something if he was hearing anything at all.

"Is anyone there? Hello?" he asked into what seemed like nothing but also felt strangely full.

"What is this? It's just... it's just me?" he asked into this odd sensation he'd never felt before.

"My thoughts... my thoughts are so loud now. Thomas Lewis... the book... my life... my existence..." Tom thought heavier into his thoughts. He was now understanding that he was no longer separate from the book nor separate from his existence in the Community Center. He was one with the other.

"What is that? It feels... deep. No... it's... it is deep. Is that an ocean? No... whatever it is it's very deep and... I think it's everywhere," Tom continued. Tom couldn't see. He only could know. He did feel the deepness surrounding him. It's a deepness that's been since the very beginning and will be there to the very end of the Community Center and existence itself.

"Who is that? Is somebody there?" Tom asked as he

felt someone speaking but not how he normally heard before. He didn't hear someone speak; he simply knew someone had words.

"What is that? What are you saying?" suddenly the boom of existence echoed through his being as he felt presence around him much more than the depth.

"Who... who just described that... who described what is happening," he asked not fully understanding yet. That's okay. It takes a moment to adjust.

"It takes a moment to adjust?"

Yes.

"What is THAT!"

Well, that's the question of the day.

"I don't see you! What are you?! Where am I?! What is this?!"

Okay, wow, a little offended. It's not as if you haven't been seeking me your entire life or anything.

"No... no... who are you? What's happening right now? I recognize you... why do I know you?"

I've been with you through everything. I'm everything that's been in between you and the story of Thomas Lewis.

"This isn't possible. I must be dreaming."

Well, spoiler alert... you don't have a head so you can't dream. You are far past having a head.

"What does that mean? How can I hear you if I don't have a head?"

Are you hearing me? Or are you only more aware of who I am?

"I... it's like I don't have any thoughts anymore... I

just...."

You're just more aware. You just *are.* You know there is a deep crashing depth all around you, but you don't have a body to see it. You simply know it's there. You know there is a presence around you that is both engulfing but equally small and interwoven between who you are.

"You're... god?"

Am I the word *god?* No. No language can really describe what I am, but you can experience what I am. A more accurate description? I am.

"Something... something is..."

Exactly. I am the *something is* your mother spoke about.

"God... the great I am... I'm so confused...."

I know. I've been with you throughout your life holding it tightly together. The deepest depths and the highest highs, I'm there.

"This is what's after death? Is this heaven?"

Well, yes.

"I'm not in hell then."

No, this is hell also.

"I'm in heaven and hell?"

You're still in the Community Center. You're still being born on Earth.

"I don't understand."

I know. But everything *is.* I am and so there is only me and what you decide to do with that.

"I can turn from you? But you just said you're everywhere?"

I am everywhere because there is only here.

"Then why let evil exist? Why all the suffering?"

Are we talking about other people's suffering or are we specifically talking about when you grieved the loss of David on the second floor?

"All of it. Why any of it? Why let David kill himself? Why let innocent people get gunned down? Why let famines and plagues and all of it happen?"

Don't stop there. Why did Kate get cancer? Why do children starve while others gorge themselves with food? Why does a father kill his wife in front of their daughter?

"What's your point?"

No. You want to play the worse game so let's play the worse game. Why do people get tortured for the way they look? Why was a man shoved into a bronze cow that heated up to hear his boiling screams on the inside? What about the man who was fed nothing but honey and milk and left in a lake until insects ate him alive? Do you want to keep playing the worse game?

"Yes actually, I do. Because I'm here and everyone on that side of the curtain wants to know why any of it happened!"

Happens.

"What?"

Happening actually.

"What are you talking about?"

You still talk like there is another side to the curtain. There isn't. Those things are happening right now Tom. There's no other side of the curtain there is only here.

"Okay fine then! Why are they happening?!"

Why do good things happen to bad people? Why do the people profiting from blood diamonds get the easy life? Why does a horrible king have a full stomach while he lets his people starve? Why do good things happen to good people? Why do bad things happen to bad people too?

"There isn't one reason for one evil or good thing?"

So often people search for the root of all evil.

"How do you stop evil?"

You're so close Tom.

"You're with me on the second floor aren't you?"

I am.

"And with me as I confront evil?"

Of course.

"Where?"

You only have to be more aware of who I am. I'm not behind the curtain. I walked through it long ago.

"Did you write my book? Did you write my life?"

No, Tom. I'm not the author of your book.

"I'm trying to understand."

I know and you're close.

"You are the something is..."

Yes.

"Evil exists on the third floor but more importantly it exists just as everything else exists in the Community Center and in the world."

Yes.

"If it exists then just like all other things, it falls on

the scale from worse to best... from evil to good. But you're outside the scale. You are the thing moving from the worst to the best. You are what can be with the lowest and the highest of people. You don't exist because you are existence. If I point at a flower I cannot say 'this flower is god'. I can't say that because well, the flower exists. And you? You're far beyond that. You are the words of our books. An author writes their book as if they were commanding a ship and following raging waters. You are what keeps the structure of the scene together. There is not one reason for why evil exists. And 'letting' it happen is void because it misunderstands what *you* are. Where all of evil and good of the world happens concurrently you are left not with many instances of evil or good but with only one decision. Only one decision made by any person who is in front of you and that's if they choose to follow you or turn away from you. You are with me confronting evil because you are with me now. You are with me when I am grieving over the loss of Kate and David because you are with me now. Any instance where I go back and read the pages of my book, I can sec you there in the words that are written. You are with me when I choose evil and when I choose to question. Every question I had was a stone's throw away to being answered if I only opened my eyes and... was more aware of who you are."

Incredible. You stumbled there a bit but that's the exciting thing about being in this place. Now, who justifies death?

"I don't know if anyone does."

You asked me why good people die. If I'm everything you said I am. Why do I let these things happen?

"Because you don't want to interfere?"

I interfere all the time. So why do I still let people die? Again, who justifies death?

"I don't understand the question."

You hate people suffering because it affects you. What you fail to understand is I know what happens to those people when they die. Death is the god of existence because you exist. One day the curtain will engulf you into a mystery. I ask for you to give up the god of death and follow me. Not because I instill fear from the threat of an eternal damnation. I ask you to follow me because I am what you say I am. So when you die, whether a perfect person or a sinful traitor, you will know with certainty who I am and death... the curtain... is nothing but a fleeting thing.

"Why does everything feel so much more intense?"

You don't have a body anymore. The veil has been lifted.

"Do you and I just talk for eternity then?"

No, in fact I'm only keeping this going for the story. There's much to do.

"What story?"

The story being read. The reader can only see what is happening on a page right now. Words being typed as they read. So they think the authors idea of the afterlife is just a void where one speaks with me for eternity. Unfortunately, there isn't a way to type out what *not* having a body actually is.

"This is the strangest and most absolute feeling I've encountered. I have so many questions."

Good! I want you to.

"I spent my entire life asking myself the big questions. What's after death? What's behind the curtain? Why the ballot? Why believe anything? I didn't trust anyone else's beliefs because how could I? I didn't know if anyone else even existed as I was. I met the representation of evil and a man who obsessed over an incomplete puzzle. All of existence goes back and forth between good and evil. It goes back and forth between wealthy and poor. But the directions left and right are only dependent on the perspective of the being they subscribe to. There is something outside of existence and non-existence. Never stop seeking. Never stop questioning and wanting the answer. Search it out, ask for it, want it. Keep going."

Simple. I like it.

"Where are we going now?"

We're already here.

www.ingramcontent.com/pod-product-compliance
Lightning Source LLC
Chambersburg PA
CBHW011801090426
42811CB00036B/2351/J

* 9 7 8 0 5 7 8 2 9 3 2 4 0 *